M000073534

PERSONAL INFORMATION

Name:

Address:

Telephone: Email:

Employer:

Address:

Telephone: Email:

MEDICAL INFORMATION

Physician: Telephone:

Allergies:

Medications:

Blood Type:

Insurer:

IN CASE OF EMERGENCY, NOTIFY

Name:

Address:

Telephone: Relationship:

ISBN 978-1-64352-907-3

Published by Barbour Publishing, Inc., 1810 Barbour Drive, Uhrichsville, Ohio 44683, www.barbourbooks.com

Our mission is to inspire the world with the life-changing message of the Bible.

Member of the
Evangelical Christian
Publishers Association

2022 PLANNER

Daily
ENCOURAGEMENT
FOR
Women

DAYMAKER
A Division of Barbour Publishing

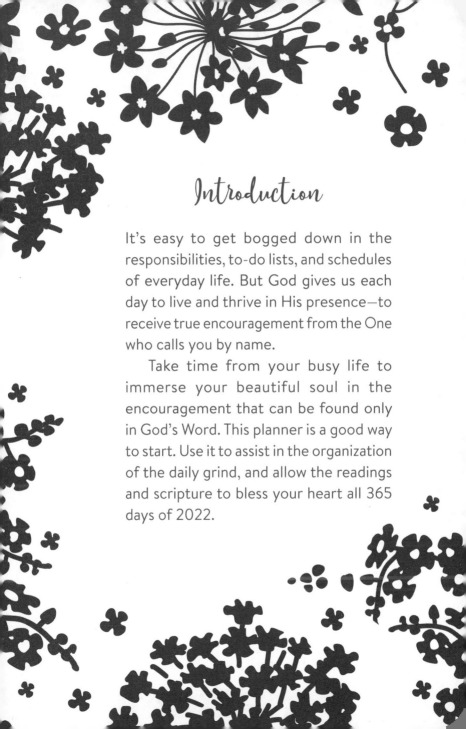

Introduction

It's easy to get bogged down in the responsibilities, to-do lists, and schedules of everyday life. But God gives us each day to live and thrive in His presence—to receive true encouragement from the One who calls you by name.

Take time from your busy life to immerse your beautiful soul in the encouragement that can be found only in God's Word. This planner is a good way to start. Use it to assist in the organization of the daily grind, and allow the readings and scripture to bless your heart all 365 days of 2022.

2022

JANUARY

S	M	T	W	T	F	S
						1
2	3	4	5	6	7	8
9	10	11	12	13	14	15
16	17	18	19	20	21	22
23	24	25	26	27	28	29
30	31					

FEBRUARY

S	M	T	W	T	F	S
		1	2	3	4	5
6	7	8	9	10	11	12
13	14	15	16	17	18	19
20	21	22	23	24	25	26
27	28					

MAY

S	M	T	W	T	F	S
1	2	3	4	5	6	7
8	9	10	11	12	13	14
15	16	17	18	19	20	21
22	23	24	25	26	27	28
29	30	31				

JUNE

S	M	T	W	T	F	S
			1	2	3	4
5	6	7	8	9	10	11
12	13	14	15	16	17	18
19	20	21	22	23	24	25
26	27	28	29	30		

SEPTEMBER

S	M	T	W	T	F	S
				1	2	3
4	5	6	7	8	9	10
11	12	13	14	15	16	17
18	19	20	21	22	23	24
25	26	27	28	29	30	

OCTOBER

S	M	T	W	T	F	S
						1
2	3	4	5	6	7	8
9	10	11	12	13	14	15
16	17	18	19	20	21	22
23	24	25	26	27	28	29
30	31					

YEAR at a GLANCE

MARCH

S	M	T	W	T	F	S
		1	2	3	4	5
6	7	8	9	10	11	12
13	14	15	16	17	18	19
20	21	22	23	24	25	26
27	28	29	30	31		

APRIL

S	M	T	W	T	F	S
					1	2
3	4	5	6	7	8	9
10	11	12	13	14	15	16
17	18	19	20	21	22	23
24	25	26	27	28	29	30

JULY

S	M	T	W	T	F	S
					1	2
3	4	5	6	7	8	9
10	11	12	13	14	15	16
17	18	19	20	21	22	23
24	25	26	27	28	29	30
31						

AUGUST

S	M	T	W	T	F	S
	1	2	3	4	5	6
7	8	9	10	11	12	13
14	15	16	17	18	19	20
21	22	23	24	25	26	27
28	29	30	31			

NOVEMBER

S	M	T	W	T	F	S
		1	2	3	4	5
6	7	8	9	10	11	12
13	14	15	16	17	18	19
20	21	22	23	24	25	26
27	28	29	30			

DECEMBER

S	M	T	W	T	F	S
				1	2	3
4	5	6	7	8	9	10
11	12	13	14	15	16	17
18	19	20	21	22	23	24
25	26	27	28	29	30	31

August 2021

SUNDAY	MONDAY	TUESDAY	WEDNESDAY
1	2	3	4
8	9	10	11
15	16	17	18
22	23	24	25
29	30	31	1

Notes

THURSDAY	FRIDAY	SATURDAY
5	6	7
12	13	14
19	20	21
26	27	28
2	3	4

....
....
....
....
....
....
....
....
....
....
....
....
....

JULY

S	M	T	W	T	F	S
				1	2	3
4	5	6	7	8	9	10
11	12	13	14	15	16	17
18	19	20	21	22	23	24
25	26	27	28	29	30	31

SEPTEMBER

S	M	T	W	T	F	S
			1	2	3	4
5	6	7	8	9	10	11
12	13	14	15	16	17	18
19	20	21	22	23	24	25
26	27	28	29	30		

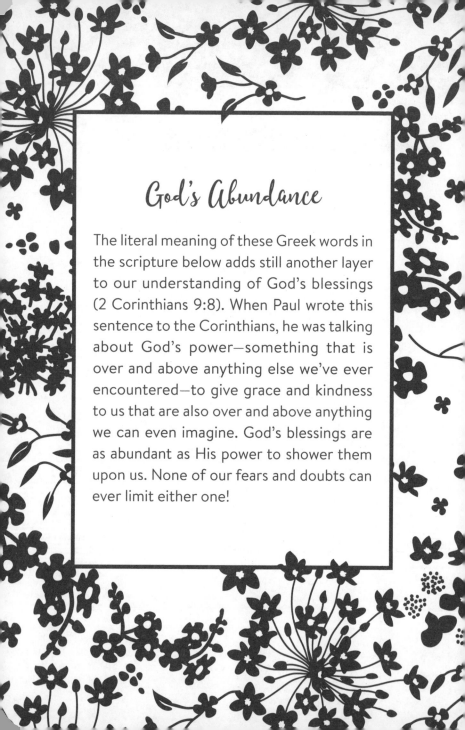

God's Abundance

The literal meaning of these Greek words in the scripture below adds still another layer to our understanding of God's blessings (2 Corinthians 9:8). When Paul wrote this sentence to the Corinthians, he was talking about God's power—something that is over and above anything else we've ever encountered—to give grace and kindness to us that are also over and above anything we can even imagine. God's blessings are as abundant as His power to shower them upon us. None of our fears and doubts can ever limit either one!

GOALS for the MONTH

God is able to bless you abundantly.
2 CORINTHIANS 9:8 NIV

August 2021

S	M	T	W	T	F	S
						1
1	2	3	4	5	6	7
8	9	10	11	12	13	14
15	16	17	18	19	20	21
22	23	24	25	26	27	28
29	30	31				

God considers you His friend.
He knows everything about you,
including your flaws,
yet He still loves you deeply.

To-Do List

- [ ]
- [ ]
- [ ]
- [ ]
- [ ]
- [ ]
- [ ]
- [ ]
- [ ]
- [ ]
- [ ]
- [ ]
- [ ]
- [ ]
- [ ]
- [ ]
- [ ]
- [ ]

SUNDAY, AUGUST 1

MONDAY, AUGUST 2

TUESDAY, AUGUST 3

WEDNESDAY, AUGUST 4

....
....
....
....
....

THURSDAY, AUGUST 5

....
....
....
....
....

FRIDAY, AUGUST 6

....
....
....
....
....

SATURDAY, AUGUST 7

....
....
....
....
....

To-Do List

.... ☐
.... ☐
.... ☐
.... ☐
.... ☐
.... ☐
.... ☐
.... ☐
.... ☐
.... ☐
.... ☐
.... ☐
.... ☐

"I'm no longer calling you servants because servants don't understand what their master is thinking and planning. No, I've named you friends because I've let you in on everything I've heard from the Father."

JOHN 15:15 MSG

August 2021

S	M	T	W	T	F	S
1	2	3	4	5	6	7
8	9	10	11	12	13	14
15	16	17	18	19	20	21
22	23	24	25	26	27	28
29	30	31				

All God's blessings, both spiritual and physical, are wrapped up in His love. Because He loves us, He will never stop blessing us. His love never fails.

To-Do List

- [ ]
- [ ]
- [ ]
- [ ]
- [ ]
- [ ]
- [ ]
- [ ]
- [ ]
- [ ]
- [ ]
- [ ]
- [ ]
- [ ]
- [ ]
- [ ]
- [ ]
- [ ]
- [ ]
- [ ]

SUNDAY, AUGUST 8

MONDAY, AUGUST 9

TUESDAY, AUGUST 10

WEDNESDAY, AUGUST 11

THURSDAY, AUGUST 12

FRIDAY, AUGUST 13

SATURDAY, AUGUST 14

I am like an olive tree, thriving in the house of God. I will always trust in God's unfailing love.

PSALM 52:8 NLT

August 2021

S	M	T	W	T	F	S
1	2	3	4	5	6	7
8	9	10	11	12	13	14
15	16	17	18	19	20	21
22	23	24	25	26	27	28
29	30	31				

God's love is perfect. It will never let us down. He never pulls away from us, no matter what we do. We are totally secure.

To-Do List

- ☐
- ☐
- ☐
- ☐
- ☐
- ☐
- ☐
- ☐
- ☐
- ☐
- ☐
- ☐
- ☐
- ☐
- ☐
- ☐
- ☐
- ☐

SUNDAY, AUGUST 15

MONDAY, AUGUST 16

TUESDAY, AUGUST 17

WEDNESDAY, AUGUST 18

THURSDAY, AUGUST 19

FRIDAY, AUGUST 20

SATURDAY, AUGUST 21

To-Do List

☐
☐
☐
☐
☐
☐
☐
☐
☐
☐
☐
☐
☐
☐
☐
☐

*Such love has no fear,
because perfect love
expels all fear. If we are
afraid, it is for fear of
punishment.*

1 JOHN 4:18 NLT

August 2021

S	M	T	W	T	F	S
1	2	3	4	5	6	7
8	9	10	11	12	13	14
15	16	17	18	19	20	21
22	23	24	25	26	27	28
29	30	31				

God is with us through every situation we face. If we need help or direction, we can trust that voice on the inside to provide us with the right way to go.

To-Do List

- ☐
- ☐
- ☐
- ☐
- ☐
- ☐
- ☐
- ☐
- ☐
- ☐
- ☐
- ☐
- ☐
- ☐
- ☐
- ☐
- ☐
- ☐
- ☐

SUNDAY, AUGUST 22

MONDAY, AUGUST 23

TUESDAY, AUGUST 24

WEDNESDAY, AUGUST 25

THURSDAY, AUGUST 26

FRIDAY, AUGUST 27

SATURDAY, AUGUST 28

To-Do List

For God has said, "I will never fail you. I will never abandon you."

<small>HEBREWS 13:5 NLT</small>

September 2021

SUNDAY	MONDAY	TUESDAY	WEDNESDAY
29	30	31	1
5	6 *Labor Day*	7	8
12	13	14	15
19	20	21	22 *First Day of Autumn*
26	27	28	29

Notes

THURSDAY	FRIDAY	SATURDAY
2	3	4
9	10	11
16	17	18
23	24	25
30	1	2

AUGUST

S	M	T	W	T	F	S
1	2	3	4	5	6	7
8	9	10	11	12	13	14
15	16	17	18	19	20	21
22	23	24	25	26	27	28
29	30	31				

OCTOBER

S	M	T	W	T	F	S
					1	2
3	4	5	6	7	8	9
10	11	12	13	14	15	16
17	18	19	20	21	22	23
24	25	26	27	28	29	30
31						

Strengthen the Hand of a Friend

When you "strengthen someone's hand," you encourage them. You speak words of affirmation; you remind them of God's faithfulness, and you urge them to immerse themselves in His grace. This Hebrew phrase from 1 Samuel 23:16 carries the idea of directing someone to be courageous despite their circumstances. Like Jonathan, King David's best friend, we all have friends who need to be encouraged. Look around. Whose hand can you strengthen today?

GOALS *for the* MONTH

And Jonathan Saul's son arose, and went to
David into the wood, and strengthened his hand in God.
1 SAMUEL 23:16 KJV

September 2021

S	M	T	W	T	F	S
			1	2	3	4
5	6	7	8	9	10	11
12	13	14	15	16	17	18
19	20	21	22	23	24	25
26	27	28	29	30		

We are God's. We belong to Him and "live and move and have our being" (Acts 17:28 NIV) in His pasture. Such comfort!

To-Do List

- ☐
- ☐
- ☐
- ☐
- ☐
- ☐
- ☐
- ☐
- ☐
- ☐
- ☐
- ☐
- ☐
- ☐
- ☐
- ☐
- ☐
- ☐
- ☐
- ☐

SUNDAY, AUGUST 29

MONDAY, AUGUST 30

TUESDAY, AUGUST 31

WEDNESDAY, SEPTEMBER 1

THURSDAY, SEPTEMBER 2

FRIDAY, SEPTEMBER 3

SATURDAY, SEPTEMBER 4

To-Do List

- [ ]
- [ ]
- [ ]
- [ ]
- [ ]
- [ ]
- [ ]
- [ ]
- [ ]
- [ ]
- [ ]
- [ ]
- [ ]
- [ ]
- [ ]
- [ ]
- [ ]

We are *His people
and the sheep
of His pasture.*
PSALM 100:3 NASB

September 2021

S	M	T	W	T	F	S
			1	2	3	4
5	6	7	8	9	10	11
12	13	14	15	16	17	18
19	20	21	22	23	24	25
26	27	28	29	30		

Your fears do not put off the Master. He can handle them. He can soothe and calm your spirit. He sees the beauty within and wants to bring it out.

To-Do List

- ☐ ....
- ☐ ....
- ☐ ....
- ☐ ....
- ☐ ....
- ☐ ....
- ☐ ....
- ☐ ....
- ☐ ....
- ☐ ....
- ☐ ....
- ☐ ....
- ☐ ....
- ☐ ....
- ☐ ....
- ☐ ....
- ☐ ....
- ☐ ....
- ☐ ....

SUNDAY, SEPTEMBER 5

MONDAY, SEPTEMBER 6   Labor Day

TUESDAY, SEPTEMBER 7

WEDNESDAY, SEPTEMBER 8

THURSDAY, SEPTEMBER 9

FRIDAY, SEPTEMBER 10

SATURDAY, SEPTEMBER 11

To-Do List

□
□
□
□
□
□
□
□
□
□
□
□
□
□
□
□
□
□
□

*I sought the LORD,
and He heard me,
and delivered me
from all my fears.*

PSALM 34:4 NKJV

September 2021

S	M	T	W	T	F	S
			1	2	3	4
5	6	7	8	9	10	11
12	13	14	15	16	17	18
19	20	21	22	23	24	25
26	27	28	29	30		

When we live in love, we are living in God. God is living in us. His blessing flows through us and out into the world.

To-Do List

- ☐ ....
- ☐ ....
- ☐ ....
- ☐ ....
- ☐ ....
- ☐ ....
- ☐ ....
- ☐ ....
- ☐ ....
- ☐ ....
- ☐ ....
- ☐ ....
- ☐ ....
- ☐ ....
- ☐ ....
- ☐ ....
- ☐ ....
- ☐ ....
- ☐ ....

SUNDAY, SEPTEMBER 12

MONDAY, SEPTEMBER 13

TUESDAY, SEPTEMBER 14

WEDNESDAY, SEPTEMBER 15

To-Do List

THURSDAY, SEPTEMBER 16

FRIDAY, SEPTEMBER 17

SATURDAY, SEPTEMBER 18

*God is love, and all who
live in love live in God,
and God lives in them.*

1 JOHN 4:16 NLT

September 2021

S	M	T	W	T	F	S
			1	2	3	4
5	6	7	8	9	10	11
12	13	14	15	16	17	18
19	20	21	22	23	24	25
26	27	28	29	30		

God is the only one who sees everything and orchestrates life in a way that only He can. Trust Him to do so.

To-Do List

- [ ]
- [ ]
- [ ]
- [ ]
- [ ]
- [ ]
- [ ]
- [ ]
- [ ]
- [ ]
- [ ]
- [ ]
- [ ]
- [ ]
- [ ]
- [ ]
- [ ]
- [ ]
- [ ]

SUNDAY, SEPTEMBER 19

MONDAY, SEPTEMBER 20

TUESDAY, SEPTEMBER 21

WEDNESDAY, SEPTEMBER 22
First Day of Autumn

THURSDAY, SEPTEMBER 23

FRIDAY, SEPTEMBER 24

SATURDAY, SEPTEMBER 25

To-Do List

☐
☐
☐
☐
☐
☐
☐
☐
☐
☐
☐
☐
☐
☐
☐
☐
☐
☐

Follow the example of those who are going to inherit God's promises because of their faith and endurance.

HEBREWS 6:12 NLT

September 2021

S	M	T	W	T	F	S
			1	2	3	4
5	6	7	8	9	10	11
12	13	14	15	16	17	18
19	20	21	22	23	24	25
26	27	28	29	30		

God's joy makes us strong, able to face the challenges of life, able to reach out to others. Just as He shares His gladness with us, we are meant to share our joy with everyone we meet.

To-Do List

☐
☐
☐
☐
☐
☐
☐
☐
☐
☐
☐
☐
☐
☐
☐
☐
☐
☐
☐

SUNDAY, SEPTEMBER 26

MONDAY, SEPTEMBER 27

TUESDAY, SEPTEMBER 28

WEDNESDAY, SEPTEMBER 29

THURSDAY, SEPTEMBER 30

FRIDAY, OCTOBER 1

SATURDAY, OCTOBER 2

"Don't be dejected and sad, for the joy of the Lord is your strength!"

NEHEMIAH 8:10 NLT

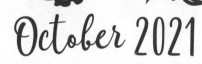

October 2021

SUNDAY	MONDAY	TUESDAY	WEDNESDAY
26	27	28	29
3	4	5	6
10	11 *Columbus Day*	12	13
17	18	19	20
24	25	26	27
31 *Halloween*			

Notes

THURSDAY	FRIDAY	SATURDAY
30	1	2
7	8	9
14	15	16
21	22	23
28	29	30

SEPTEMBER

S	M	T	W	T	F	S
			1	2	3	4
5	6	7	8	9	10	11
12	13	14	15	16	17	18
19	20	21	22	23	24	25
26	27	28	29	30		

NOVEMBER

S	M	T	W	T	F	S
	1	2	3	4	5	6
7	8	9	10	11	12	13
14	15	16	17	18	19	20
21	22	23	24	25	26	27
28	29	30				

Past and Present Beauty

Every memory you have is colored by your perception, your emotion, your vantage point. Your memories, to a large degree, are you. We women treasure memories of special days, events, and emotions.

Today, God wants you to know that you are as beautiful to Him as on that long-ago day when your hair was fluffed and your dress was princess-like. You wish for past beauty, but the reality is that, to Him, you are always lovely.

GOALS for the MONTH

_But Mary quietly treasured these things
in her heart and often thought about them._
LUKE 2:19 TLB

October 2021

S	M	T	W	T	F	S
					1	2
3	4	5	6	7	8	9
10	11	12	13	14	15	16
17	18	19	20	21	22	23
24	25	26	27	28	29	30
31						

You're in God's school of grace. He invites you to get in sync with Him and learn how to do things His way. It's the way to beautiful living.

To-Do List

- [ ]
- [ ]
- [ ]
- [ ]
- [ ]
- [ ]
- [ ]
- [ ]
- [ ]
- [ ]
- [ ]
- [ ]
- [ ]
- [ ]
- [ ]
- [ ]
- [ ]
- [ ]

SUNDAY, OCTOBER 3

MONDAY, OCTOBER 4

TUESDAY, OCTOBER 5

WEDNESDAY, OCTOBER 6

THURSDAY, OCTOBER 7

FRIDAY, OCTOBER 8

SATURDAY, OCTOBER 9

To-Do List

☐
☐
☐
☐
☐
☐
☐
☐
☐
☐
☐
☐
☐
☐
☐
☐
☐
☐
☐
☐
☐

"Take My yoke upon you and learn from Me."
MATTHEW 11:29 NKJV

October 2021

S	M	T	W	T	F	S
					1	2
3	4	5	6	7	8	9
10	11	12	13	14	15	16
17	18	19	20	21	22	23
24	25	26	27	28	29	30
31						

To-Do List

- [ ]
- [ ]
- [ ]
- [ ]
- [ ]
- [ ]
- [ ]
- [ ]
- [ ]
- [ ]
- [ ]
- [ ]
- [ ]
- [ ]
- [ ]
- [ ]
- [ ]

We *have* all been blessed by God in ways that make us sing! Even if we can't carry a tune, He's glad to hear our voices lifted up in praise.

SUNDAY, OCTOBER 10

MONDAY, OCTOBER 11 *Columbus Day*

TUESDAY, OCTOBER 12

WEDNESDAY, OCTOBER 13

THURSDAY, OCTOBER 14

FRIDAY, OCTOBER 15

SATURDAY, OCTOBER 16

☐
☐
☐
☐
☐
☐
☐
☐
☐
☐
☐
☐
☐
☐
☐
☐
☐
☐

They shall lift up their voice, they shall sing for the majesty of the LORD, they shall cry aloud.

ISAIAH 24:14 KJV

October 2021

S	M	T	W	T	F	S
					1	2
3	4	5	6	7	8	9
10	11	12	13	14	15	16
17	18	19	20	21	22	23
24	25	26	27	28	29	30
31						

When we pray in faith, anything can happen. Pray the Word, and watch it come to life!

To-Do List

- [ ] ....
- [ ] ....
- [ ] ....
- [ ] ....
- [ ] ....
- [ ] ....
- [ ] ....
- [ ] ....
- [ ] ....
- [ ] ....
- [ ] ....
- [ ] ....
- [ ] ....
- [ ] ....
- [ ] ....
- [ ] ....
- [ ] ....
- [ ] ....
- [ ] ....
- [ ] ....
- [ ] ....

SUNDAY, OCTOBER 17

MONDAY, OCTOBER 18

TUESDAY, OCTOBER 19

WEDNESDAY, OCTOBER 20

THURSDAY, OCTOBER 21

FRIDAY, OCTOBER 22

SATURDAY, OCTOBER 23

To-Do List

- [ ]
- [ ]
- [ ]
- [ ]
- [ ]
- [ ]
- [ ]
- [ ]
- [ ]
- [ ]
- [ ]
- [ ]
- [ ]
- [ ]

Elijah was as human as we are, and yet when he prayed earnestly that no rain would fall, none fell for three and a half years! Then, when he prayed again, the sky sent down rain and the earth began to yield its crops.

JAMES 5:17–18 NLT

October 2021

S	M	T	W	T	F	S
					1	2
3	4	5	6	7	8	9
10	11	12	13	14	15	16
17	18	19	20	21	22	23
24	25	26	27	28	29	30
31						

If you don't know what to pray, go to the Bible. There you'll find prayers to say that will encourage you in the process.

To-Do List

- [ ]
- [ ]
- [ ]
- [ ]
- [ ]
- [ ]
- [ ]
- [ ]
- [ ]
- [ ]
- [ ]
- [ ]
- [ ]
- [ ]
- [ ]
- [ ]
- [ ]
- [ ]

SUNDAY, OCTOBER 24

MONDAY, OCTOBER 25

TUESDAY, OCTOBER 26

WEDNESDAY, OCTOBER 27

THURSDAY, OCTOBER 28

FRIDAY, OCTOBER 29

SATURDAY, OCTOBER 30

☐
☐
☐
☐
☐
☐
☐
☐
☐
☐
☐
☐
☐
☐
☐
☐
☐

*That he would grant
you, according to
the riches of his glory,
to be strengthened
with might by his Spirit
in the inner man.*

EPHESIANS 3:16 KJV

November 2021

SUNDAY	MONDAY	TUESDAY	WEDNESDAY
31	1	2 *Election Day*	3
7 *Daylight Saving Time Ends*	8	9	10
14	15	16	17
21	22	23	24
28 *Hanukkah Begins at Sundown*	29	30	1

Notes

THURSDAY	FRIDAY	SATURDAY
4	5	6
11 *Veterans Day*	12	13
18	19	20
25 *Thanksgiving Day*	26	27
2	3	4

....

....

....

....

....

....

....

....

....

....

....

....

OCTOBER

S	M	T	W	T	F	S
					1	2
3	4	5	6	7	8	9
10	11	12	13	14	15	16
17	18	19	20	21	22	23
24	25	26	27	28	29	30
31						

DECEMBER

S	M	T	W	T	F	S
			1	2	3	4
5	6	7	8	9	10	11
12	13	14	15	16	17	18
19	20	21	22	23	24	25
26	27	28	29	30	31	

Travels

Pack your bag and go!

There is exhilaration in seeing new places, eating different foods, and walking unknown paths. Those of us who like to wander a bit may be assured that the magnificence of every exotic place on earth is only a shadow compared to the beauty our God built in the very essence of who we are.

Whether you're sitting on a plane or by your own fireplace, think about that right now.

GOALS for the MONTH

_He shall have dominion also from sea to sea,
and from the River to the ends of the earth._

PSALM 72:8 NKJV

November 2021

S	M	T	W	T	F	S
	1	2	3	4	5	6
7	8	9	10	11	12	13
14	15	16	17	18	19	20
21	22	23	24	25	26	27
28	29	30				

> Knowing God precedes us into the future, we can let go of all our worries. We can go in peace.

To-Do List

- [ ]
- [ ]
- [ ]
- [ ]
- [ ]
- [ ]
- [ ]
- [ ]
- [ ]
- [ ]
- [ ]
- [ ]
- [ ]
- [ ]
- [ ]
- [ ]
- [ ]
- [ ]

SUNDAY, OCTOBER 31 — Halloween

MONDAY, NOVEMBER 1

TUESDAY, NOVEMBER 2 — Election Day

WEDNESDAY, NOVEMBER 3

THURSDAY, NOVEMBER 4

FRIDAY, NOVEMBER 5

SATURDAY, NOVEMBER 6

To-Do List

"Go in peace.
Your journey has
the LORD's approval."
JUDGES 18:6 NIV

November 2021

S	M	T	W	T	F	S
	1	2	3	4	5	6
7	8	9	10	11	12	13
14	15	16	17	18	19	20
21	22	23	24	25	26	27
28	29	30				

We have been healed, body and soul. All the broken pieces of our hearts have been put back together. In Christ, we have been made whole.

To-Do List

- [ ] ....
- [ ] ....
- [ ] ....
- [ ] ....
- [ ] ....
- [ ] ....
- [ ] ....
- [ ] ....
- [ ] ....
- [ ] ....
- [ ] ....
- [ ] ....
- [ ] ....
- [ ] ....
- [ ] ....
- [ ] ....
- [ ] ....
- [ ] ....
- [ ] ....

SUNDAY, NOVEMBER 7
Daylight Saving Time Ends

MONDAY, NOVEMBER 8

TUESDAY, NOVEMBER 9

WEDNESDAY, NOVEMBER 10

THURSDAY, NOVEMBER 11
Veterans Day

FRIDAY, NOVEMBER 12

SATURDAY, NOVEMBER 13

To-Do List

☐
☐
☐
☐
☐
☐
☐
☐
☐
☐
☐
☐
☐
☐
☐
☐
☐
☐
☐
☐

*And He said to her,
"Daughter, your faith
has made you well;
go in peace and
be cured."*

MARK 5:34 NASB

November 2021

S	M	T	W	T	F	S
	1	2	3	4	5	6
7	8	9	10	11	12	13
14	15	16	17	18	19	20
21	22	23	24	25	26	27
28	29	30				

When our work is done for God,
it's full of meaning; it is fruitful.
So let's throw ourselves into our jobs
this week and watch Him bless them.

To-Do List

☐
☐
☐
☐
☐
☐
☐
☐
☐
☐
☐
☐
☐
☐
☐
☐
☐
☐
☐

SUNDAY, NOVEMBER 14

MONDAY, NOVEMBER 15

TUESDAY, NOVEMBER 16

WEDNESDAY, NOVEMBER 17

THURSDAY, NOVEMBER 18

FRIDAY, NOVEMBER 19

SATURDAY, NOVEMBER 20

To-Do List

☐
☐
☐
☐
☐
☐
☐
☐
☐
☐
☐
☐
☐
☐
☐
☐
☐
☐
☐

*Throw yourselves into
the work of the Master,
confident that nothing
you do for him is a
waste of time or effort.*
1 CORINTHIANS 15:58 MSG

November 2021

S	M	T	W	T	F	S
	1	2	3	4	5	6
7	8	9	10	11	12	13
14	15	16	17	18	19	20
21	22	23	24	25	26	27
28	29	30				

When self-doubt surfaces, think about what makes you special. Know that God has made you as He did for a reason. You can embrace your beauty.

To-Do List

- [ ] ....
- [ ] ....
- [ ] ....
- [ ] ....
- [ ] ....
- [ ] ....
- [ ] ....
- [ ] ....
- [ ] ....
- [ ] ....
- [ ] ....
- [ ] ....
- [ ] ....
- [ ] ....
- [ ] ....
- [ ] ....
- [ ] ....
- [ ] ....

SUNDAY, NOVEMBER 21

MONDAY, NOVEMBER 22

TUESDAY, NOVEMBER 23

WEDNESDAY, NOVEMBER 24

....
....
....
....
....

THURSDAY, NOVEMBER 25
Thanksgiving Day

....
....
....
....

FRIDAY, NOVEMBER 26

....
....
....
....
....

SATURDAY, NOVEMBER 27

....
....
....
....
....

To-Do List

☐
☐
☐
☐
☐
☐
☐
☐
☐
☐
☐
☐
☐
☐
☐
☐
☐
☐

"Before I formed you in the womb I knew you, and before you were born I consecrated you; I appointed you a prophet to the nations."

JEREMIAH 1:5 ESV

December 2021

SUNDAY	MONDAY	TUESDAY	WEDNESDAY
28	29	30	1
5	6	7	8
12	13	14	15
19	20	21 *First Day of Winter*	22
26	27	28	29

Notes

THURSDAY	FRIDAY	SATURDAY
2	3	4
9	10	11
16	17	18
23	24 *Christmas Eve*	25 *Christmas Day*
30	31 *New Year's Eve*	1

NOVEMBER

S	M	T	W	T	F	S
	1	2	3	4	5	6
7	8	9	10	11	12	13
14	15	16	17	18	19	20
21	22	23	24	25	26	27
28	29	30				

JANUARY

S	M	T	W	T	F	S
						1
2	3	4	5	6	7	8
9	10	11	12	13	14	15
16	17	18	19	20	21	22
23	24	25	26	27	28	29
30	31					

It Has Already Been Given to Us

Stop the struggle. We have already been given all that we need for this life and the one to come. Christ has arranged for it all. Our job is just to stay connected to Him. We connect through prayer, meditation, and Bible reading. We see His face as we serve. We already have all the tools necessary to accomplish His will in our lives. We just need to use them.

GOALS for the MONTH

....

....

....

....

....

....

....

....

....

....

....

....

....

....

....

....

....

*Everything that goes into a life of pleasing God
has been miraculously given to us by getting to know,
personally and intimately, the One who invited us to God.*

2 PETER 1:3 MSG

December 2021

S	M	T	W	T	F	S
			1	2	3	4
5	6	7	8	9	10	11
12	13	14	15	16	17	18
19	20	21	22	23	24	25
26	27	28	29	30	31	

Through Christ, you have the right to ask God for help and care. He speaks to you; He gives you happiness and health; He protects you; and He gives you countless gifts!

To-Do List

- ☐
- ☐
- ☐
- ☐
- ☐
- ☐
- ☐
- ☐
- ☐
- ☐
- ☐
- ☐
- ☐
- ☐
- ☐
- ☐
- ☐
- ☐
- ☐

SUNDAY, NOVEMBER 28
Hanukkah Begins at Sundown

MONDAY, NOVEMBER 29

TUESDAY, NOVEMBER 30

WEDNESDAY, DECEMBER 1

THURSDAY, DECEMBER 2

FRIDAY, DECEMBER 3

SATURDAY, DECEMBER 4

To-Do List

*"I will be with you
and bless you."*
GENESIS 26:3 NLT

December 2021

S	M	T	W	T	F	S
			1	2	3	4
5	6	7	8	9	10	11
12	13	14	15	16	17	18
19	20	21	22	23	24	25
26	27	28	29	30	31	

Our prayers enable us to access God in heaven. What a privilege! If you want something from heaven to come to Earth, pray. Entreat God to make it happen.

To-Do List

- [ ]
- [ ]
- [ ]
- [ ]
- [ ]
- [ ]
- [ ]
- [ ]
- [ ]
- [ ]
- [ ]
- [ ]
- [ ]
- [ ]
- [ ]
- [ ]
- [ ]
- [ ]

SUNDAY, DECEMBER 5

MONDAY, DECEMBER 6

TUESDAY, DECEMBER 7

WEDNESDAY, DECEMBER 8

....
....
....
....
....

THURSDAY, DECEMBER 9

....
....
....
....
....

FRIDAY, DECEMBER 10

....
....
....
....
....

SATURDAY, DECEMBER 11

....
....
....
....
....

To-Do List

- [ ]
- [ ]
- [ ]
- [ ]
- [ ]
- [ ]
- [ ]
- [ ]
- [ ]
- [ ]
- [ ]
- [ ]
- [ ]
- [ ]
- [ ]
- [ ]
- [ ]
- [ ]

"May your Kingdom come soon. May your will be done on earth, as it is in heaven."

MATTHEW 6:10 NLT

December 2021

S	M	T	W	T	F	S
			1	2	3	4
5	6	7	8	9	10	11
12	13	14	15	16	17	18
19	20	21	22	23	24	25
26	27	28	29	30	31	

In the same way, God set the stars in the sky (Genesis 1:17) and a rainbow in the clouds (Genesis 9:13), He has literally placed us on a course before we were even born. Being set aside for a very specific purpose shows God's love for us.

To-Do List

SUNDAY, DECEMBER 12

MONDAY, DECEMBER 13

TUESDAY, DECEMBER 14

WEDNESDAY, DECEMBER 15

THURSDAY, DECEMBER 16

FRIDAY, DECEMBER 17

SATURDAY, DECEMBER 18

To-Do List

"Before I formed you in the womb I knew you, before you were born I set you apart."

JEREMIAH 1:5 NIV

December 2021

S	M	T	W	T	F	S
			1	2	3	4
5	6	7	8	9	10	11
12	13	14	15	16	17	18
19	20	21	22	23	24	25
26	27	28	29	30	31	

The Bible has the power to do amazing things in us. If you have trouble reading the Word, ask the Holy Spirit to help. He'll make the Bible come alive for you!

To-Do List

- .... ☐
- .... ☐
- .... ☐
- .... ☐
- .... ☐
- .... ☐
- .... ☐
- .... ☐
- .... ☐
- .... ☐
- .... ☐
- .... ☐
- .... ☐
- .... ☐
- .... ☐
- .... ☐
- .... ☐
- .... ☐

SUNDAY, DECEMBER 19

MONDAY, DECEMBER 20

TUESDAY, DECEMBER 21
First Day of Winter

WEDNESDAY, DECEMBER 22

THURSDAY, DECEMBER 23

FRIDAY, DECEMBER 24   *Christmas Eve*

SATURDAY, DECEMBER 25
Christmas Day

To-Do List

*All Scripture is inspired
by God and is useful to
teach us what is true and
to make us realize what
is wrong in our lives. It
corrects us when we are
wrong and teaches us
to do what is right.*

2 TIMOTHY 3:16 NLT

December 2021

S	M	T	W	T	F	S
			1	2	3	4
5	6	7	8	9	10	11
12	13	14	15	16	17	18
19	20	21	22	23	24	25
26	27	28	29	30	31	

God is patient with us,
no matter how many times we fall
on our faces, no matter how long
we take to learn something. He never
stops believing in us. He's willing to
put up with us for as long as it takes!

To-Do List

- [ ]
- [ ]
- [ ]
- [ ]
- [ ]
- [ ]
- [ ]
- [ ]
- [ ]
- [ ]
- [ ]
- [ ]
- [ ]
- [ ]
- [ ]
- [ ]
- [ ]
- [ ]
- [ ]

SUNDAY, DECEMBER 26

MONDAY, DECEMBER 27

TUESDAY, DECEMBER 28

WEDNESDAY, DECEMBER 29

THURSDAY, DECEMBER 30

FRIDAY, DECEMBER 31 *New Year's Eve*

SATURDAY, JANUARY 1 *New Year's Day*

To-Do List

☐
☐
☐
☐
☐
☐
☐
☐
☐
☐
☐
☐
☐
☐
☐
☐
☐
☐

Love is patient, love is kind. . .believes all things, hopes all things, endures all things.

1 CORINTHIANS 13:4, 7 NASB

January 2022

SUNDAY	MONDAY	TUESDAY	WEDNESDAY
26	27	28	29
2	3	4	5
9	10	11	12
16	17 *Martin Luther King Jr. Day*	18	19
23 / 30	24 / 31	25	26

Notes

THURSDAY	FRIDAY	SATURDAY
30	31	1 *New Year's Day*
6	7	8
13	14	15
20	21	22
27	28	29

....
....
....
....
....
....
....
....
....
....
....
....

DECEMBER

S	M	T	W	T	F	S
			1	2	3	4
5	6	7	8	9	10	11
12	13	14	15	16	17	18
19	20	21	22	23	24	25
26	27	28	29	30	31	

FEBRUARY

S	M	T	W	T	F	S
		1	2	3	4	5
6	7	8	9	10	11	12
13	14	15	16	17	18	19
20	21	22	23	24	25	26
27	28					

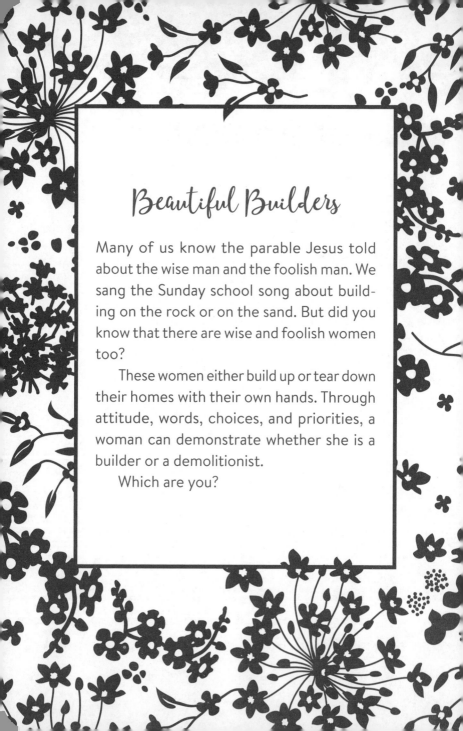

Beautiful Builders

Many of us know the parable Jesus told about the wise man and the foolish man. We sang the Sunday school song about building on the rock or on the sand. But did you know that there are wise and foolish women too?

These women either build up or tear down their homes with their own hands. Through attitude, words, choices, and priorities, a woman can demonstrate whether she is a builder or a demolitionist.

Which are you?

GOALS for the MONTH

....

....

....

....

....

....

....

....

....

....

....

....

....

....

....

....

....

The wise woman builds her house, but the
foolish pulls it down with her hands.

PROVERBS 14:1 NKJV

January 2022

S	M	T	W	T	F	S
						1
2	3	4	5	6	7	8
9	10	11	12	13	14	15
16	17	18	19	20	21	22
23	24	25	26	27	28	29
30	31					

God's blessings are never limited by human problems—and He does nothing by half measures!

To-Do List

- [ ]
- [ ]
- [ ]
- [ ]
- [ ]
- [ ]
- [ ]
- [ ]
- [ ]
- [ ]
- [ ]
- [ ]
- [ ]
- [ ]
- [ ]
- [ ]
- [ ]
- [ ]

SUNDAY, JANUARY 2

MONDAY, JANUARY 3

TUESDAY, JANUARY 4

WEDNESDAY, JANUARY 5

THURSDAY, JANUARY 6

FRIDAY, JANUARY 7

SATURDAY, JANUARY 8

☐
☐
☐
☐
☐
☐
☐
☐
☐
☐
☐
☐
☐
☐
☐
☐
☐
☐
☐
☐

*I am exceeding joyful
in all our tribulation.*
2 CORINTHIANS 7:4 KJV

January 2022

S	M	T	W	T	F	S
						1
2	3	4	5	6	7	8
9	10	11	12	13	14	15
16	17	18	19	20	21	22
23	24	25	26	27	28	29
30	31					

Trust God to show you the path He wants you to walk. It may look different from others, but as long as it is aligned with God's Word, follow your heart.

To-Do List

- [ ] ....
- [ ] ....
- [ ] ....
- [ ] ....
- [ ] ....
- [ ] ....
- [ ] ....
- [ ] ....
- [ ] ....
- [ ] ....
- [ ] ....
- [ ] ....
- [ ] ....
- [ ] ....
- [ ] ....
- [ ] ....
- [ ] ....
- [ ] ....

SUNDAY, JANUARY 9

MONDAY, JANUARY 10

TUESDAY, JANUARY 11

WEDNESDAY, JANUARY 12

THURSDAY, JANUARY 13

FRIDAY, JANUARY 14

SATURDAY, JANUARY 15

*Then Saul gave David
his own armor. . . .
"I can't go in these,"
[David] protested to
Saul. "I'm not used to
them." So David took
them off again.*
1 SAMUEL 17:38–39 NLT

January 2022

S	M	T	W	T	F	S
						1
2	3	4	5	6	7	8
9	10	11	12	13	14	15
16	17	18	19	20	21	22
23	24	25	26	27	28	29
30	31					

Today, whatever season of the year it is outside, you are on God's mind. In the spring, He likes you in pastels. In the summer, He delights in your joy of going barefoot. In the fall, He looks at you with love in your sweater and scarf. And in the winter, He smiles at the snowflakes in your hair.

To-Do List

- [ ] ....
- [ ] ....
- [ ] ....
- [ ] ....
- [ ] ....
- [ ] ....
- [ ] ....
- [ ] ....
- [ ] ....
- [ ] ....
- [ ] ....
- [ ] ....
- [ ] ....
- [ ] ....
- [ ] ....
- [ ] ....
- [ ] ....
- [ ] ....

SUNDAY, JANUARY 16

MONDAY, JANUARY 17
Martin Luther King Jr. Day

TUESDAY, JANUARY 18

WEDNESDAY, JANUARY 19

THURSDAY, JANUARY 20

FRIDAY, JANUARY 21

SATURDAY, JANUARY 22

To-Do List

☐
☐
☐
☐
☐
☐
☐
☐
☐
☐
☐
☐
☐
☐
☐
☐
☐
☐

*"As long as the
earth remains, there
will be springtime and
harvest, cold and heat,
winter and summer,
day and night."*

GENESIS 8:22 TLB

January 2022

S	M	T	W	T	F	S
						1
2	3	4	5	6	7	8
9	10	11	12	13	14	15
16	17	18	19	20	21	22
23	24	25	26	27	28	29
30	31					

The heavenly Father teaches us—
and teaching is a process that's often
long and slow. We have so much to
learn, but God sees our lives clearly,
and He has promised to teach us
everything we need to know.

To-Do List

- [ ] ....
- [ ] ....
- [ ] ....
- [ ] ....
- [ ] ....
- [ ] ....
- [ ] ....
- [ ] ....
- [ ] ....
- [ ] ....
- [ ] ....
- [ ] ....
- [ ] ....
- [ ] ....
- [ ] ....
- [ ] ....
- [ ] ....

SUNDAY, JANUARY 23

MONDAY, JANUARY 24

TUESDAY, JANUARY 25

WEDNESDAY, JANUARY 26

THURSDAY, JANUARY 27

FRIDAY, JANUARY 28

SATURDAY, JANUARY 29

To-Do List

☐
☐
☐
☐
☐
☐
☐
☐
☐
☐
☐
☐
☐
☐
☐
☐
☐
☐
☐
☐

*I will instruct you and
teach you in the way
which you should go;
I will advise you with
My eye upon you.*

PSALM 32:8 NASB

February 2022

SUNDAY	MONDAY	TUESDAY	WEDNESDAY
30	31	1	2
6	7	8	9
13	14 _Valentine's Day_	15	16
20	21 _Presidents' Day_	22	23
27	28	1	2

Notes

THURSDAY	FRIDAY	SATURDAY
3	4	5
10	11	12
17	18	19
24	25	26
3	4	5

....
....
....
....
....
....
....
....
....
....
....
....

JANUARY

S	M	T	W	T	F	S
						1
2	3	4	5	6	7	8
9	10	11	12	13	14	15
16	17	18	19	20	21	22
23	24	25	26	27	28	29
30	31					

MARCH

S	M	T	W	T	F	S
		1	2	3	4	5
6	7	8	9	10	11	12
13	14	15	16	17	18	19
20	21	22	23	24	25	26
27	28	29	30	31		

Wordless Praise

Deer and woodchucks, chipmunks and rabbits, snakes and spiders, dragonflies and prairie dogs: each creature in its own way praises and honors God. Wordlessly, even without human intelligence and reasoning, they show us that God provides for His creation even in the most barren lands. His blessings reach into the wild, secret places. He forgets none of His creation and blesses it all.

GOALS for the MONTH

The beast of the field shall honour me. . .because I
give waters in the wilderness, and rivers in the desert.
Isaiah 43:20 kjv

February 2022

S	M	T	W	T	F	S
		1	2	3	4	5
6	7	8	9	10	11	12
13	14	15	16	17	18	19
20	21	22	23	24	25	26
27	28					

God wants to be part of every rainy day you have. Trust Him when the clouds start to roll in. He is still watching out for you.

To-Do List

- [ ]
- [ ]
- [ ]
- [ ]
- [ ]
- [ ]
- [ ]
- [ ]
- [ ]
- [ ]
- [ ]
- [ ]
- [ ]
- [ ]
- [ ]
- [ ]
- [ ]
- [ ]

SUNDAY, JANUARY 30

MONDAY, JANUARY 31

TUESDAY, FEBRUARY 1

WEDNESDAY, FEBRUARY 2

THURSDAY, FEBRUARY 3

FRIDAY, FEBRUARY 4

SATURDAY, FEBRUARY 5

To-Do List

☐
☐
☐
☐
☐
☐
☐
☐
☐
☐
☐
☐
☐
☐
☐
☐
☐
☐

"He gives rain on the earth, and sends waters on the fields."

JOB 5:10 NKJV

February 2022

S	M	T	W	T	F	S
		1	2	3	4	5
6	7	8	9	10	11	12
13	14	15	16	17	18	19
20	21	22	23	24	25	26
27	28					

God wants us to be lovely through and through. He has given us His Word to show us where we need His power to make us that way.

To-Do List

- [ ]
- [ ]
- [ ]
- [ ]
- [ ]
- [ ]
- [ ]
- [ ]
- [ ]
- [ ]
- [ ]
- [ ]
- [ ]
- [ ]
- [ ]
- [ ]
- [ ]
- [ ]

SUNDAY, FEBRUARY 6

MONDAY, FEBRUARY 7

TUESDAY, FEBRUARY 8

WEDNESDAY, FEBRUARY 9

THURSDAY, FEBRUARY 10

FRIDAY, FEBRUARY 11

SATURDAY, FEBRUARY 12

To-Do List

☐
☐
☐
☐
☐
☐
☐
☐
☐
☐
☐
☐
☐
☐
☐

For the word of God is living and powerful, and sharper than any two-edged sword, piercing even to the division of soul and spirit, and of joints and marrow, and is a discerner of the thoughts and intents of the heart.

HEBREWS 4:12 NKJV

February 2022

S	M	T	W	T	F	S
		1	2	3	4	5
6	7	8	9	10	11	12
13	14	15	16	17	18	19
20	21	22	23	24	25	26
27	28					

Enjoying the blessings of nature is a form of worship. The awe and delight we feel when we see a towering mountain, a storm-tossed ocean, or a field of wildflowers can turn our hearts to God.

To-Do List

- ☐
- ☐
- ☐
- ☐
- ☐
- ☐
- ☐
- ☐
- ☐
- ☐
- ☐
- ☐
- ☐
- ☐
- ☐
- ☐
- ☐
- ☐
- ☐

SUNDAY, FEBRUARY 13

MONDAY, FEBRUARY 14
Valentine's Day

TUESDAY, FEBRUARY 15

WEDNESDAY, FEBRUARY 16

THURSDAY, FEBRUARY 17

FRIDAY, FEBRUARY 18

SATURDAY, FEBRUARY 19

To-Do List

*"Worthy are You,
our Lord and our God,
to receive glory and
honor and power;
for You created all
things, and because of
Your will they existed,
and were created."*

REVELATION 4:11 NASB

February 2022

S	M	T	W	T	F	S
		1	2	3	4	5
6	7	8	9	10	11	12
13	14	15	16	17	18	19
20	21	22	23	24	25	26
27	28					

One way we reflect Jesus to the world is by looking for other people's needs and doing everything we can to meet them. Ask God: Whose needs can I meet today?

To-Do List

- [ ] ....
- [ ] ....
- [ ] ....
- [ ] ....
- [ ] ....
- [ ] ....
- [ ] ....
- [ ] ....
- [ ] ....
- [ ] ....
- [ ] ....
- [ ] ....
- [ ] ....
- [ ] ....
- [ ] ....
- [ ] ....
- [ ] ....
- [ ] ....

SUNDAY, FEBRUARY 20

MONDAY, FEBRUARY 21
Presidents' Day

TUESDAY, FEBRUARY 22

WEDNESDAY, FEBRUARY 23

....

....

....

....

....

THURSDAY, FEBRUARY 24

....

....

....

....

....

FRIDAY, FEBRUARY 25

....

....

....

....

....

SATURDAY, FEBRUARY 26

....

....

....

....

....

To-Do List

- [ ]
- [ ]
- [ ]
- [ ]
- [ ]
- [ ]
- [ ]
- [ ]
- [ ]
- [ ]
- [ ]
- [ ]
- [ ]
- [ ]
- [ ]
- [ ]
- [ ]
- [ ]
- [ ]

For the LORD gives wisdom; from his mouth come knowledge and understanding.

PROVERBS 2:6 NIV

March 2022

SUNDAY	MONDAY	TUESDAY	WEDNESDAY
27	28	1	2 *Ash Wednesday*
6	7	8	9
13 *Daylight Saving Time Begins*	14	15	16
20 *First Day of Spring*	21	22	23
27	28	29	30

Notes

THURSDAY	FRIDAY	SATURDAY
3	4	5
10	11	12
17	18	19
St. Patrick's Day		
24	25	26
31	1	2

....
....
....
....
....
....
....
....
....
....
....
....

FEBRUARY

S	M	T	W	T	F	S
		1	2	3	4	5
6	7	8	9	10	11	12
13	14	15	16	17	18	19
20	21	22	23	24	25	26
27	28					

APRIL

S	M	T	W	T	F	S
					1	2
3	4	5	6	7	8	9
10	11	12	13	14	15	16
17	18	19	20	21	22	23
24	25	26	27	28	29	30

The Blessing of Friendship

When things are going our way, we may be tempted to think we are so strong that we don't need anyone's help. We may consider ourselves so spiritually mature that we can go it alone, "just me and the Lord." But sooner or later, all of us face times when everything seems to fall apart. We can't cope with life, and even our faith falters. When a friend quietly offers us her hand, that's the moment we truly understand the blessing of friendship!

GOALS for the MONTH

*A friend loves at all times, and a
brother is born for adversity.*
PROVERBS 17:17 NASB

March 2022

S	M	T	W	T	F	S
		1	2	3	4	5
6	7	8	9	10	11	12
13	14	15	16	17	18	19
20	21	22	23	24	25	26
27	28	29	30	31		

God hasn't called us to judge other people's decisions. Our job is to love them, recognize we don't understand their situation, and give them grace upon grace for what they are facing.

To-Do List

- [ ]
- [ ]
- [ ]
- [ ]
- [ ]
- [ ]
- [ ]
- [ ]
- [ ]
- [ ]
- [ ]
- [ ]
- [ ]
- [ ]
- [ ]
- [ ]
- [ ]

SUNDAY, FEBRUARY 27

MONDAY, FEBRUARY 28

TUESDAY, MARCH 1

WEDNESDAY, MARCH 2 *Ash Wednesday*

THURSDAY, MARCH 3

FRIDAY, MARCH 4

SATURDAY, MARCH 5

"Don't pick on people, jump on their failures, criticize their faults— unless, of course, you want the same treatment. That critical spirit has a way of boomeranging."

MATTHEW 7:1–2 MSG

March 2022

S	M	T	W	T	F	S
		1	2	3	4	5
6	7	8	9	10	11	12
13	14	15	16	17	18	19
20	21	22	23	24	25	26
27	28	29	30	31		

Thank God for the people you know casually and for each stranger you pass on the street. Thank Him even for the difficult people you encounter! Each and every one of them can be a vehicle for God's blessing to flow into your life.

To-Do List

- ☐
- ☐
- ☐
- ☐
- ☐
- ☐
- ☐
- ☐
- ☐
- ☐
- ☐
- ☐
- ☐
- ☐
- ☐
- ☐
- ☐
- ☐

SUNDAY, MARCH 6

MONDAY, MARCH 7

TUESDAY, MARCH 8

WEDNESDAY, MARCH 9

THURSDAY, MARCH 10

FRIDAY, MARCH 11

SATURDAY, MARCH 12

To-Do List

- [ ]
- [ ]
- [ ]
- [ ]
- [ ]
- [ ]
- [ ]
- [ ]
- [ ]
- [ ]
- [ ]
- [ ]
- [ ]
- [ ]
- [ ]
- [ ]
- [ ]
- [ ]
- [ ]

*I always thank
my God for you.*
1 CORINTHIANS 1:4 NLT

March 2022

S	M	T	W	T	F	S
		1	2	3	4	5
6	7	8	9	10	11	12
13	14	15	16	17	18	19
20	21	22	23	24	25	26
27	28	29	30	31		

One day we will see Jesus face-to-face, and our eyes will be fully opened to see the majesty of that glory revealed in us as we never saw it on earth.

To-Do List

- [ ]
- [ ]
- [ ]
- [ ]
- [ ]
- [ ]
- [ ]
- [ ]
- [ ]
- [ ]
- [ ]
- [ ]
- [ ]
- [ ]
- [ ]
- [ ]
- [ ]
- [ ]
- [ ]

SUNDAY, MARCH 13
Daylight Saving Time Begins

MONDAY, MARCH 14

TUESDAY, MARCH 15

WEDNESDAY, MARCH 16

THURSDAY, MARCH 17
St. Patrick's Day

FRIDAY, MARCH 18

SATURDAY, MARCH 19

*For now we see
through a glass, darkly;
but then face to face:
now I know in part; but
then shall I know even
as also I am known.*

1 CORINTHIANS 13:12 KJV

March 2022

S	M	T	W	T	F	S
		1	2	3	4	5
6	7	8	9	10	11	12
13	14	15	16	17	18	19
20	21	22	23	24	25	26
27	28	29	30	31		

The Bible says that God put eternity into our hearts. Deep inside our innermost beings we yearn for all that eternity holds, all its abundance and beauty. Only God can give us the deepest, real desires of our hearts.

To-Do List

- ☐ ....
- ☐ ....
- ☐ ....
- ☐ ....
- ☐ ....
- ☐ ....
- ☐ ....
- ☐ ....
- ☐ ....
- ☐ ....
- ☐ ....
- ☐ ....
- ☐ ....
- ☐ ....
- ☐ ....
- ☐ ....
- ☐ ....

SUNDAY, MARCH 20
First Day of Spring

MONDAY, MARCH 21

TUESDAY, MARCH 22

WEDNESDAY, MARCH 23

THURSDAY, MARCH 24

FRIDAY, MARCH 25

SATURDAY, MARCH 26

- [ ]
- [ ]
- [ ]
- [ ]
- [ ]
- [ ]
- [ ]
- [ ]
- [ ]
- [ ]
- [ ]
- [ ]
- [ ]
- [ ]
- [ ]
- [ ]
- [ ]
- [ ]
- [ ]

*Take delight in the LORD,
and he will give you the
desires of your heart.*
PSALM 37:4 NIV

March 2022

S	M	T	W	T	F	S
		1	2	3	4	5
6	7	8	9	10	11	12
13	14	15	16	17	18	19
20	21	22	23	24	25	26
27	28	29	30	31		

Aim to keep your ears tuned in to the voice that matters most: our heavenly Father. As you tune in to Him and tune out others, you'll hear the Lord's voice more clearly.

To-Do List

☐
☐
☐
☐
☐
☐
☐
☐
☐
☐
☐
☐
☐
☐
☐
☐
☐
☐

SUNDAY, MARCH 27

MONDAY, MARCH 28

TUESDAY, MARCH 29

WEDNESDAY, MARCH 30

THURSDAY, MARCH 31

FRIDAY, APRIL 1

SATURDAY, APRIL 2

To-Do List

*Their loyalty is divided
between God and
the world, and they
are unstable in
everything they do.*

JAMES 1:8 NLT

April 2022

SUNDAY	MONDAY	TUESDAY	WEDNESDAY
27	28	29	30
3	4	5	6
10 *Palm Sunday*	11	12	13
17 *Easter*	18	19	20
24	25	26	27

Notes

THURSDAY	FRIDAY	SATURDAY
31	1	2
7	8	9
14	15 *Passover Begins at Sundown* *Good Friday*	16
21	22	23
28	29	30

MARCH

S	M	T	W	T	F	S
		1	2	3	4	5
6	7	8	9	10	11	12
13	14	15	16	17	18	19
20	21	22	23	24	25	26
27	28	29	30	31		

MAY

S	M	T	W	T	F	S
1	2	3	4	5	6	7
8	9	10	11	12	13	14
15	16	17	18	19	20	21
22	23	24	25	26	27	28
29	30	31				

His Parting Gift

The most significant gift anyone could ever be given is the peace of God. The night before He died, Christ made sure His disciples understood that truth. He promised to never leave them alone. He promised to be with them in all circumstances. And He promised them a gift, a confident assurance that could structure and give meaning to their entire life. He promised them (and us) His peace. Are you leaning into it today?

GOALS for the MONTH

·····
·····
·····
·····
·····
·····
·····
·····
·····
·····
·····
·····
·····
·····
·····
·····
·····
·····
·····
·····
·····
·····
·····
·····
·····
·····
·····

*"That's my parting gift to you. Peace. I don't
leave you the way you're used to being left—
feeling abandoned, bereft. So don't be upset."*
JOHN 14:27 MSG

April 2022

S	M	T	W	T	F	S
					1	2
3	4	5	6	7	8	9
10	11	12	13	14	15	16
17	18	19	20	21	22	23
24	25	26	27	28	29	30

Some tears are ones of joy; but mostly, tears denote sorrow. And God is going to eliminate sorrow from our eternal existence. Won't that be beautiful?

To-Do List

☐
☐
☐
☐
☐
☐
☐
☐
☐
☐
☐
☐
☐
☐
☐
☐
☐
☐
☐

SUNDAY, APRIL 3

MONDAY, APRIL 4

TUESDAY, APRIL 5

WEDNESDAY, APRIL 6

THURSDAY, APRIL 7

FRIDAY, APRIL 8

SATURDAY, APRIL 9

*And God shall wipe
away all tears from
their eyes; and there
shall be no more death,
neither sorrow, nor
crying, neither shall
there be any more pain:
for the former things
are passed away.*

REVELATION 21:4 KJV

April 2022

S	M	T	W	T	F	S
					1	2
3	4	5	6	7	8	9
10	11	12	13	14	15	16
17	18	19	20	21	22	23
24	25	26	27	28	29	30

The message of the Gospel all wrapped up in a nutshell: God loves you. . .God gives you His Son. . .through Jesus you have life. . .in Him you'll never die.

To-Do List

- [ ]
- [ ]
- [ ]
- [ ]
- [ ]
- [ ]
- [ ]
- [ ]
- [ ]
- [ ]
- [ ]
- [ ]
- [ ]
- [ ]
- [ ]
- [ ]
- [ ]
- [ ]

SUNDAY, APRIL 10 — Palm Sunday

MONDAY, APRIL 11

TUESDAY, APRIL 12

WEDNESDAY, APRIL 13

....
....
....
....
....

THURSDAY, APRIL 14

....
....
....
....
....

FRIDAY, APRIL 15
Passover Begins at Sundown
Good Friday

....
....
....

SATURDAY, APRIL 16

....
....
....
....
....

To-Do List

☐
☐
☐
☐
☐
☐
☐
☐
☐
☐
☐
☐
☐
☐
☐
☐
☐
☐

For God so loved the world, that he gave his only begotten Son, that whosoever believeth in him should not perish, but have everlasting life.

JOHN 3:16 KJV

April 2022

S	M	T	W	T	F	S
					1	2
3	4	5	6	7	8	9
10	11	12	13	14	15	16
17	18	19	20	21	22	23
24	25	26	27	28	29	30

You are a living testimony to God's power to bring beauty to a human life. Let others read a clear testimony from your life today.

To-Do List

- [ ]
- [ ]
- [ ]
- [ ]
- [ ]
- [ ]
- [ ]
- [ ]
- [ ]
- [ ]
- [ ]
- [ ]
- [ ]
- [ ]
- [ ]
- [ ]
- [ ]
- [ ]

SUNDAY, APRIL 17 — Easter

MONDAY, APRIL 18

TUESDAY, APRIL 19

WEDNESDAY, APRIL 20

THURSDAY, APRIL 21

FRIDAY, APRIL 22

SATURDAY, APRIL 23

*For the invisible things
of him from the creation
of the world are clearly
seen, being understood
by the things that are
made, even his eternal
power and Godhead;
so that they are
without excuse.*

ROMANS 1:20 KJV

April 2022

S	M	T	W	T	F	S
					1	2
3	4	5	6	7	8	9
10	11	12	13	14	15	16
17	18	19	20	21	22	23
24	25	26	27	28	29	30

Staying true to God's purposes requires time in His Word. Let's start turning our eyes away from the worthless stuff and spend time with our Savior.

To-Do List

- ☐
- ☐
- ☐
- ☐
- ☐
- ☐
- ☐
- ☐
- ☐
- ☐
- ☐
- ☐
- ☐
- ☐
- ☐
- ☐
- ☐
- ☐

SUNDAY, APRIL 24

MONDAY, APRIL 25

TUESDAY, APRIL 26

WEDNESDAY, APRIL 27

THURSDAY, APRIL 28

FRIDAY, APRIL 29

SATURDAY, APRIL 30

☐
☐
☐
☐
☐
☐
☐
☐
☐
☐
☐
☐
☐
☐
☐
☐
☐
☐

*Turn my eyes away
from worthless things;
preserve my life
according to your word.*
PSALM 119:37 NIV

May 2022

SUNDAY	MONDAY	TUESDAY	WEDNESDAY
1	2	3	4
8 *Mother's Day*	9	10	11
15	16	17	18
22	23	24	25
29	30 *Memorial Day*	31	1

Notes

....
....
....
....
....
....
....
....
....
....
....
....

THURSDAY	FRIDAY	SATURDAY
5 *National Day of Prayer*	6	7
12	13	14
19	20	21
26	27	28
2	3	4

APRIL

S	M	T	W	T	F	S
					1	2
3	4	5	6	7	8	9
10	11	12	13	14	15	16
17	18	19	20	21	22	23
24	25	26	27	28	29	30

JUNE

S	M	T	W	T	F	S
			1	2	3	4
5	6	7	8	9	10	11
12	13	14	15	16	17	18
19	20	21	22	23	24	25
26	27	28	29	30		

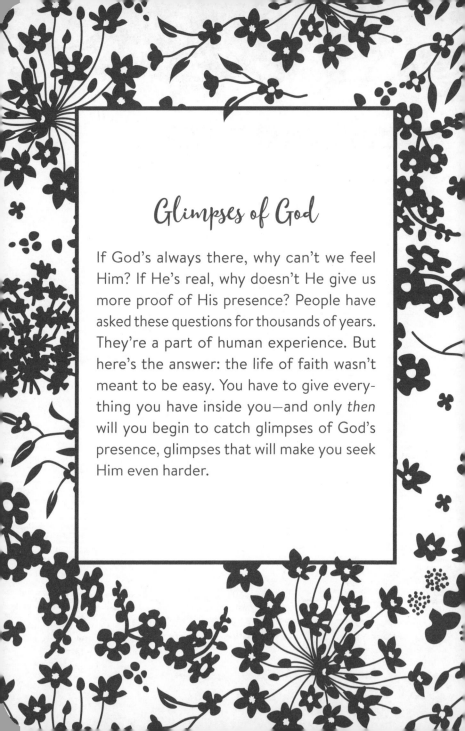

Glimpses of God

If God's always there, why can't we feel Him? If He's real, why doesn't He give us more proof of His presence? People have asked these questions for thousands of years. They're a part of human experience. But here's the answer: the life of faith wasn't meant to be easy. You have to give everything you have inside you—and only *then* will you begin to catch glimpses of God's presence, glimpses that will make you seek Him even harder.

GOALS for the MONTH

"You will seek Me and find Me when you
search for Me with all your heart."
JEREMIAH 29:13 NASB

May 2022

S	M	T	W	T	F	S
1	2	3	4	5	6	7
8	9	10	11	12	13	14
15	16	17	18	19	20	21
22	23	24	25	26	27	28
29	30	31				

As Christians, we plan our lives the way we think they should play out. The reality, though, is that we can prepare all day long, but in the end, the path to victory is given by the Lord.

To-Do List

- [ ]
- [ ]
- [ ]
- [ ]
- [ ]
- [ ]
- [ ]
- [ ]
- [ ]
- [ ]
- [ ]
- [ ]
- [ ]
- [ ]
- [ ]
- [ ]
- [ ]
- [ ]
- [ ]

SUNDAY, MAY 1

MONDAY, MAY 2

TUESDAY, MAY 3

WEDNESDAY, MAY 4

THURSDAY, MAY 5
National Day of Prayer

FRIDAY, MAY 6

SATURDAY, MAY 7

To-Do List

*The horse is prepared
for the day of battle,
but the victory
belongs to the LORD.*
PROVERBS 21:31 NLT

May 2022

S	M	T	W	T	F	S
1	2	3	4	5	6	7
8	9	10	11	12	13	14
15	16	17	18	19	20	21
22	23	24	25	26	27	28
29	30	31				

Be salt. Be light. Spread the delightful savor of His splendor, and shine brightly on everyone near you.

To-Do List

- [ ]
- [ ]
- [ ]
- [ ]
- [ ]
- [ ]
- [ ]
- [ ]
- [ ]
- [ ]
- [ ]
- [ ]
- [ ]
- [ ]
- [ ]
- [ ]
- [ ]
- [ ]

SUNDAY, MAY 8 — *Mother's Day*

MONDAY, MAY 9

TUESDAY, MAY 10

WEDNESDAY, MAY 11

THURSDAY, MAY 12

FRIDAY, MAY 13

SATURDAY, MAY 14

To-Do List

☐
☐
☐
☐
☐
☐
☐
☐
☐
☐
☐
☐
☐
☐

"You are the salt of the earth; but if the salt loses its flavor, how shall it be seasoned? It is then good for nothing but to be thrown out and trampled underfoot by men. You are the light of the world. A city that is set on a hill cannot be hidden."

MATTHEW 5:13–14 NKJV

May 2022

S	M	T	W	T	F	S
1	2	3	4	5	6	7
8	9	10	11	12	13	14
15	16	17	18	19	20	21
22	23	24	25	26	27	28
29	30	31				

God is here with you, living in the midst of your life. You make Him happy, so happy that He's singing you love songs. Let His love calm and comfort your heart.

To-Do List

- ☐
- ☐
- ☐
- ☐
- ☐
- ☐
- ☐
- ☐
- ☐
- ☐
- ☐
- ☐
- ☐
- ☐
- ☐
- ☐
- ☐
- ☐
- ☐

SUNDAY, MAY 15

MONDAY, MAY 16

TUESDAY, MAY 17

WEDNESDAY, MAY 18

THURSDAY, MAY 19

FRIDAY, MAY 20

SATURDAY, MAY 21

"The LORD your God is
living among you. He is
a mighty savior. He will
take delight in you with
gladness. With his love,
he will calm all your
fears. He will rejoice over
you with joyful songs."

ZEPHANIAH 3:17 NLT

May 2022

S	M	T	W	T	F	S
1	2	3	4	5	6	7
8	9	10	11	12	13	14
15	16	17	18	19	20	21
22	23	24	25	26	27	28
29	30	31				

Even though God is *always* with us, we perceive our life as a journey toward Him, with stopping places along the way. Again and again, God meets us anew—all the way to heaven.

To-Do List

- [ ]
- [ ]
- [ ]
- [ ]
- [ ]
- [ ]
- [ ]
- [ ]
- [ ]
- [ ]
- [ ]
- [ ]
- [ ]
- [ ]
- [ ]
- [ ]
- [ ]
- [ ]
- [ ]

SUNDAY, MAY 22

MONDAY, MAY 23

TUESDAY, MAY 24

WEDNESDAY, MAY 25

THURSDAY, MAY 26

FRIDAY, MAY 27

SATURDAY, MAY 28

To-Do List

- [ ]
- [ ]
- [ ]
- [ ]
- [ ]
- [ ]
- [ ]
- [ ]
- [ ]
- [ ]
- [ ]
- [ ]
- [ ]
- [ ]
- [ ]
- [ ]
- [ ]

June 2022

SUNDAY	MONDAY	TUESDAY	WEDNESDAY
29	30	31	1
5	6	7	8
12	13	14 *Flag Day*	15
19 *Father's Day*	20	21 *First Day of Summer*	22
26	27	28	29

Notes

THURSDAY	FRIDAY	SATURDAY
2	3	4
9	10	11
16	17	18
23	24	25
30	1	2

MAY

S	M	T	W	T	F	S
1	2	3	4	5	6	7
8	9	10	11	12	13	14
15	16	17	18	19	20	21
22	23	24	25	26	27	28
29	30	31				

JULY

S	M	T	W	T	F	S
					1	2
3	4	5	6	7	8	9
10	11	12	13	14	15	16
17	18	19	20	21	22	23
24	25	26	27	28	29	30
31						

Fabulous You

You were made according to a pattern. No random fusion of DNA brought you into this world. Your parents may or may not have "planned" your creation, but God did. And while the little embryo that you once were was forming in that hidden place, God watched and waited until His masterpiece was ready to enter the outside world. And when the moment arrived, He knew you were beautiful. And you still are.

GOALS for the MONTH

------

*My frame was not hidden from You when I was being formed
in secret [and] intricately and curiously wrought [as if
embroidered with various colors] in the depths of
the earth [a region of darkness and mystery].*
PSALM 139:15 AMPC

June 2022

S	M	T	W	T	F	S
			1	2	3	4
5	6	7	8	9	10	11
12	13	14	15	16	17	18
19	20	21	22	23	24	25
26	27	28	29	30		

Nothing you do—or don't do—
will ever take away your standing
of righteousness with God. Live
with confidence that you have
been made righteous in Him!

To-Do List

- [ ]
- [ ]
- [ ]
- [ ]
- [ ]
- [ ]
- [ ]
- [ ]
- [ ]
- [ ]
- [ ]
- [ ]
- [ ]
- [ ]
- [ ]
- [ ]
- [ ]
- [ ]

SUNDAY, MAY 29

MONDAY, MAY 30 — Memorial Day

TUESDAY, MAY 31

WEDNESDAY, JUNE 1

....

....

....

....

....

THURSDAY, JUNE 2

....

....

....

....

....

FRIDAY, JUNE 3

....

....

....

....

SATURDAY, JUNE 4

....

....

....

....

....

☐
☐
☐
☐
☐
☐
☐
☐
☐
☐
☐
☐
☐
☐
☐
☐
☐
☐

Therefore, since we have been justified by faith, we have peace with God through our Lord Jesus Christ.

ROMANS 5:1 ESV

June 2022

S	M	T	W	T	F	S
			1	2	3	4
5	6	7	8	9	10	11
12	13	14	15	16	17	18
19	20	21	22	23	24	25
26	27	28	29	30		

We deserve the wrath of God, but because of His mercy (literally, His compassion), we are saved. That reality gives enormous direction to our lives. As the old hymn says, "Saved, how I love to proclaim it, saved by the blood of the lamb, His child and forever I am!"

To-Do List

- [ ]
- [ ]
- [ ]
- [ ]
- [ ]
- [ ]
- [ ]
- [ ]
- [ ]
- [ ]
- [ ]
- [ ]
- [ ]
- [ ]
- [ ]
- [ ]
- [ ]
- [ ]

SUNDAY, JUNE 5

MONDAY, JUNE 6

TUESDAY, JUNE 7

WEDNESDAY, JUNE 8

To-Do List

THURSDAY, JUNE 9

FRIDAY, JUNE 10

SATURDAY, JUNE 11

*He saved us, not
because of righteous
things we had done, but
because of his mercy.*

TITUS 3:5 NIV

June 2022

S	M	T	W	T	F	S
			1	2	3	4
5	6	7	8	9	10	11
12	13	14	15	16	17	18
19	20	21	22	23	24	25
26	27	28	29	30		

You have been gifted with a spiritual ability, a blessing to bring to the body of Christ. Look for it. Discover the beautiful offering of service that is uniquely yours to give.

To-Do List

☐
☐
☐
☐
☐
☐
☐
☐
☐
☐
☐
☐
☐
☐
☐
☐
☐
☐

SUNDAY, JUNE 12

MONDAY, JUNE 13

TUESDAY, JUNE 14 — Flag Day

WEDNESDAY, JUNE 15

THURSDAY, JUNE 16

FRIDAY, JUNE 17

SATURDAY, JUNE 18

There are diversities of gifts, but the same Spirit. There are differences of ministries, but the same Lord. And there are diversities of activities, but it is the same God who works all in all. But the manifestation of the Spirit is given to each one for the profit of all.

1 Corinthians 12:4–7 NKJV

June 2022

S	M	T	W	T	F	S
			1	2	3	4
5	6	7	8	9	10	11
12	13	14	15	16	17	18
19	20	21	22	23	24	25
26	27	28	29	30		

God cares for you and knows
the situation you are facing.
Rest in Him; He'll take care of you.

To-Do List

- [ ]
- [ ]
- [ ]
- [ ]
- [ ]
- [ ]
- [ ]
- [ ]
- [ ]
- [ ]
- [ ]
- [ ]
- [ ]
- [ ]
- [ ]
- [ ]
- [ ]
- [ ]

SUNDAY, JUNE 19 — *Father's Day*

MONDAY, JUNE 20

TUESDAY, JUNE 21
First Day of Summer

WEDNESDAY, JUNE 22

THURSDAY, JUNE 23

FRIDAY, JUNE 24

SATURDAY, JUNE 25

To-Do List

☐
☐
☐
☐
☐
☐
☐
☐
☐
☐
☐
☐
☐
☐

"And which of you by being anxious can add a single hour to his span of life? . . . But if God so clothes the grass of the field, which today is alive and tomorrow is thrown into the oven, will he not much more clothe you?"

MATTHEW 6:27, 30 ESV

June 2022

S	M	T	W	T	F	S
			1	2	3	4
5	6	7	8	9	10	11
12	13	14	15	16	17	18
19	20	21	22	23	24	25
26	27	28	29	30		

God sees the big picture of our lives as well as everyone else in the world. Our job is to bring Him our prayers and cares, and then trust Him to answer.

To-Do List

- [ ]
- [ ]
- [ ]
- [ ]
- [ ]
- [ ]
- [ ]
- [ ]
- [ ]
- [ ]
- [ ]
- [ ]
- [ ]
- [ ]
- [ ]
- [ ]
- [ ]
- [ ]
- [ ]

SUNDAY, JUNE 26

MONDAY, JUNE 27

TUESDAY, JUNE 28

WEDNESDAY, JUNE 29

THURSDAY, JUNE 30

FRIDAY, JULY 1

SATURDAY, JULY 2

Be still before the LORD and wait patiently for him; fret not yourself over the one who prospers in his way, over the man who carries out evil devices!

PSALM 37:7 ESV

July 2022

SUNDAY	MONDAY	TUESDAY	WEDNESDAY
26	27	28	29
3	4 *Independence Day*	5	6
10	11	12	13
17	18	19	20
24 / 31	25	26	27

Notes

....
....
....
....
....
....
....
....
....
....
....

THURSDAY	FRIDAY	SATURDAY
30	1	2
7	8	9
14	15	16
21	22	23
28	29	30

JUNE

S	M	T	W	T	F	S
			1	2	3	4
5	6	7	8	9	10	11
12	13	14	15	16	17	18
19	20	21	22	23	24	25
26	27	28	29	30		

AUGUST

S	M	T	W	T	F	S
	1	2	3	4	5	6
7	8	9	10	11	12	13
14	15	16	17	18	19	20
21	22	23	24	25	26	27
28	29	30	31			

Reliable

When we talk about God's love, it's not just a pretty phrase or some lofty theological concept. The Greek word in 1 John 4:16 translated here as *know* implies firsthand experience. We know God's love because it touches us personally. The more we allow ourselves to experience His love, the more we will be able to trust that love. We can put our full weight on it, knowing that God will never jerk it out from under us. How could He, when His very nature is love?

GOALS for the MONTH

....

....

....

....

....

....

....

....

....

....

....

....

....

....

....

....

....

We know and rely on the love
God has for us. God is love.
1 JOHN 4:16 NIV

July 2022

S	M	T	W	T	F	S
					1	2
3	4	5	6	7	8	9
10	11	12	13	14	15	16
17	18	19	20	21	22	23
24	25	26	27	28	29	30
31						

The Son of God loves you infinitely, unconditionally, with all His heart. What a blessing! The only thing He asks in return is that you make His love your home—that you seek out the place where your heart is close to His.

To-Do List

- ☐
- ☐
- ☐
- ☐
- ☐
- ☐
- ☐
- ☐
- ☐
- ☐
- ☐
- ☐
- ☐
- ☐
- ☐
- ☐
- ☐
- ☐
- ☐

SUNDAY, JULY 3

MONDAY, JULY 4 · Independence Day

TUESDAY, JULY 5

WEDNESDAY, JULY 6

THURSDAY, JULY 7

FRIDAY, JULY 8

SATURDAY, JULY 9

*"Just as the Father
has loved Me, I also
have loved you;
remain in My love."*

JOHN 15:9 NASB

July 2022

S	M	T	W	T	F	S
					1	2
3	4	5	6	7	8	9
10	11	12	13	14	15	16
17	18	19	20	21	22	23
24	25	26	27	28	29	30
31						

There is joy that runs after us with open arms. Even when we are deep in depression, wandering down dark and dreary paths, it catches up with us. Its presence—God's presence—chases away all our sadness.

To-Do List

- [ ]
- [ ]
- [ ]
- [ ]
- [ ]
- [ ]
- [ ]
- [ ]
- [ ]
- [ ]
- [ ]
- [ ]
- [ ]
- [ ]
- [ ]
- [ ]
- [ ]
- [ ]

SUNDAY, JULY 10

MONDAY, JULY 11

TUESDAY, JULY 12

WEDNESDAY, JULY 13

THURSDAY, JULY 14

FRIDAY, JULY 15

SATURDAY, JULY 16

*Gladness and joy
will overtake them,
and sorrow and
sighing will flee away.*

ISAIAH 35:10 NIV

July 2022

S	M	T	W	T	F	S
					1	2
3	4	5	6	7	8	9
10	11	12	13	14	15	16
17	18	19	20	21	22	23
24	25	26	27	28	29	30
31						

God wants us to trust Him with our secrets. He wants to show us the beauty of being known and loved and redeemed by His grace.

To-Do List

- ☐ ....
- ☐ ....
- ☐ ....
- ☐ ....
- ☐ ....
- ☐ ....
- ☐ ....
- ☐ ....
- ☐ ....
- ☐ ....
- ☐ ....
- ☐ ....
- ☐ ....
- ☐ ....
- ☐ ....
- ☐ ....
- ☐ ....
- ☐ ....

SUNDAY, JULY 17

MONDAY, JULY 18

TUESDAY, JULY 19

WEDNESDAY, JULY 20

THURSDAY, JULY 21

FRIDAY, JULY 22

SATURDAY, JULY 23

For He knows the secrets of the heart.
PSALM 44:21 NKJV

July 2022

S	M	T	W	T	F	S
					1	2
3	4	5	6	7	8	9
10	11	12	13	14	15	16
17	18	19	20	21	22	23
24	25	26	27	28	29	30
31						

No amount of worry can alter circumstances. Only prayer can! Bring that situation to God and leave it with Him.

To-Do List

- [ ]
- [ ]
- [ ]
- [ ]
- [ ]
- [ ]
- [ ]
- [ ]
- [ ]
- [ ]
- [ ]
- [ ]
- [ ]
- [ ]
- [ ]
- [ ]
- [ ]
- [ ]

SUNDAY, JULY 24

MONDAY, JULY 25

TUESDAY, JULY 26

WEDNESDAY, JULY 27

THURSDAY, JULY 28

FRIDAY, JULY 29

SATURDAY, JULY 30

☐
☐
☐
☐
☐
☐
☐
☐
☐
☐
☐
☐
☐
☐
☐
☐
☐

*Don't worry about
anything; instead, pray
about everything. Tell
God what you need,
and thank him for
all he has done.*

PHILIPPIANS 4:6 NLT

August 2022

SUNDAY	MONDAY	TUESDAY	WEDNESDAY
31	1	2	3
7	8	9	10
14	15	16	17
21	22	23	24
28	29	30	31

Notes

THURSDAY	FRIDAY	SATURDAY
4	5	6
11	12	13
18	19	20
25	26	27
1	2	3

....

....

....

....

....

....

....

....

....

....

....

....

JULY

S	M	T	W	T	F	S
					1	2
3	4	5	6	7	8	9
10	11	12	13	14	15	16
17	18	19	20	21	22	23
24	25	26	27	28	29	30
31						

SEPTEMBER

S	M	T	W	T	F	S
				1	2	3
4	5	6	7	8	9	10
11	12	13	14	15	16	17
18	19	20	21	22	23	24
25	26	27	28	29	30	

Satisfaction in Our Work

When God included work in His plan for our lives, He never envisioned the endless stress that accompanies much of our modern work world. The term *satisfaction* in the scripture on the next page implies rest or the ability to lay something down and walk away. When we work with the right attitude and for the right reasons, it just feels good, and we can walk away with a real sense of godly accomplishment.

GOALS for the MONTH

....
....
....
....
....
....
....
....
....
....
....
....
....
....
....
....
....
....

A person can do nothing better than to eat
and drink and find satisfaction in their own toil.
ECCLESIASTES 2:24 NIV

August 2022

S	M	T	W	T	F	S
	1	2	3	4	5	6
7	8	9	10	11	12	13
14	15	16	17	18	19	20
21	22	23	24	25	26	27
28	29	30	31			

Whatever your past, God will use it to create beauty in you if you give Him permission to filter it with His grace. Use your maturity to be done with self-pity, and make a choice to let the healing begin.

To-Do List

☐
☐
☐
☐
☐
☐
☐
☐
☐
☐
☐
☐
☐
☐
☐

SUNDAY, JULY 31

MONDAY, AUGUST 1

TUESDAY, AUGUST 2

WEDNESDAY, AUGUST 3

THURSDAY, AUGUST 4

FRIDAY, AUGUST 5

SATURDAY, AUGUST 6

☐
☐
☐
☐
☐
☐
☐
☐
☐
☐
☐
☐
☐
☐
☐

When I was a child,
I talked like a child,
I thought like a child,
I reasoned like a child;
now that I have become
a man, I am done with
childish ways and have
put them aside.

1 CORINTHIANS 13:11 AMPC

August 2022

S	M	T	W	T	F	S
	1	2	3	4	5	6
7	8	9	10	11	12	13
14	15	16	17	18	19	20
21	22	23	24	25	26	27
28	29	30	31			

What happens when you turn a light on in a dark room? Darkness has no option; it must leave. When you shine your light for Jesus, darkness has no option as well. It must leave. Go shine your light to the world.

To-Do List

- ☐
- ☐
- ☐
- ☐
- ☐
- ☐
- ☐
- ☐
- ☐
- ☐
- ☐
- ☐
- ☐
- ☐
- ☐
- ☐
- ☐
- ☐

SUNDAY, AUGUST 7

MONDAY, AUGUST 8

TUESDAY, AUGUST 9

WEDNESDAY, AUGUST 10

THURSDAY, AUGUST 11

FRIDAY, AUGUST 12

SATURDAY, AUGUST 13

To-Do List

Ye are the light of the world. A city that is set on an hill cannot be hid. . . . Let your light so shine before men, that they may see your good works, and glorify your Father which is in heaven.

MATTHEW 5:14, 16 KJV

August 2022

S	M	T	W	T	F	S
	1	2	3	4	5	6
7	8	9	10	11	12	13
14	15	16	17	18	19	20
21	22	23	24	25	26	27
28	29	30	31			

If you have given your heart to Jesus, you are more than part of the collective bride of Christ; you are an individual, beloved by Him, beautified through His sacrifice on the cross.

To-Do List

- [ ]
- [ ]
- [ ]
- [ ]
- [ ]
- [ ]
- [ ]
- [ ]
- [ ]
- [ ]
- [ ]
- [ ]
- [ ]
- [ ]
- [ ]
- [ ]
- [ ]
- [ ]

SUNDAY, AUGUST 14

MONDAY, AUGUST 15

TUESDAY, AUGUST 16

WEDNESDAY, AUGUST 17

THURSDAY, AUGUST 18

FRIDAY, AUGUST 19

SATURDAY, AUGUST 20

To-Do List

*So that he could give
her to himself as a
glorious Church without
a single spot or wrinkle
or any other blemish,
being holy and without
a single fault.*

EPHESIANS 5:27 TLB

August 2022

S	M	T	W	T	F	S
	1	2	3	4	5	6
7	8	9	10	11	12	13
14	15	16	17	18	19	20
21	22	23	24	25	26	27
28	29	30	31			

When we feed the hungry or help the sick, our world brightens and our energy level soars. Reaching out in service turns on the light for all of us.

To-Do List

- [ ]
- [ ]
- [ ]
- [ ]
- [ ]
- [ ]
- [ ]
- [ ]
- [ ]
- [ ]
- [ ]
- [ ]
- [ ]
- [ ]
- [ ]
- [ ]
- [ ]
- [ ]
- [ ]
- [ ]

SUNDAY, AUGUST 21

MONDAY, AUGUST 22

TUESDAY, AUGUST 23

WEDNESDAY, AUGUST 24

THURSDAY, AUGUST 25

FRIDAY, AUGUST 26

SATURDAY, AUGUST 27

To-Do List

☐
☐
☐
☐
☐
☐
☐
☐
☐
☐
☐
☐
☐
☐
☐
☐

*"And if you offer
yourself to the hungry
and satisfy the need of
the afflicted, then your
light will rise in darkness,
and your gloom will
become like midday."*

ISAIAH 58:10 NASB

August 2022

S	M	T	W	T	F	S
	1	2	3	4	5	6
7	8	9	10	11	12	13
14	15	16	17	18	19	20
21	22	23	24	25	26	27
28	29	30	31			

If you belong to Christ, you are surrounded by His power and covered from anything outside of His will for you. He has you in the palm of His hand. Like a princess protected by a knight, you are safe.

To-Do List

- [ ] ....
- [ ] ....
- [ ] ....
- [ ] ....
- [ ] ....
- [ ] ....
- [ ] ....
- [ ] ....
- [ ] ....
- [ ] ....
- [ ] ....
- [ ] ....
- [ ] ....
- [ ] ....
- [ ] ....
- [ ] ....
- [ ] ....
- [ ] ....
- [ ] ....

SUNDAY, AUGUST 28

MONDAY, AUGUST 29

TUESDAY, AUGUST 30

WEDNESDAY, AUGUST 31

THURSDAY, SEPTEMBER 1

FRIDAY, SEPTEMBER 2

SATURDAY, SEPTEMBER 3

☐
☐
☐
☐
☐
☐
☐
☐
☐
☐
☐
☐
☐
☐
☐
☐
☐
☐
☐
☐

You, who are kept by the power of God through faith for salvation.

1 PETER 1:4–5 NKJV

September 2022

SUNDAY	MONDAY	TUESDAY	WEDNESDAY
28	29	30	31
4	5 *Labor Day*	6	7
11	12	13	14
18	19	20	21
25	26	27	28

Notes

THURSDAY	FRIDAY	SATURDAY
1	2	3
8	9	10
15	16	17
22	23	24
First Day of Autumn		
29	30	1

....
....
....
....
....
....
....
....
....
....
....
....

Holy Adrenaline

God living inside us through His Holy Spirit gives us power, a kind of holy adrenaline. You may be a single woman. You may have lost a spouse. You may be surrounded by children and their needs. You may be in a difficult marriage. Whatever the place, God has promised you the resources through His grace to live there.

GOALS *for the* MONTH

As you live this new life, we pray that you will be strengthened from God's boundless resources, so that you will find yourselves able to pass through any experience and endure it with courage.
COLOSSIANS 1:11 PHILLIPS

September 2022

S	M	T	W	T	F	S
				1	2	3
4	5	6	7	8	9	10
11	12	13	14	15	16	17
18	19	20	21	22	23	24
25	26	27	28	29	30	

When you feel the sun on your face or moonlight pours through your window, think of God's light shining in your heart. When you see water spilling clear and bright out of the earth, remember that Jesus is a well of living water springing up within you.

To-Do List

SUNDAY, SEPTEMBER 4

MONDAY, SEPTEMBER 5 — Labor Day

TUESDAY, SEPTEMBER 6

WEDNESDAY, SEPTEMBER 7

THURSDAY, SEPTEMBER 8

FRIDAY, SEPTEMBER 9

SATURDAY, SEPTEMBER 10

To-Do List

- [ ]
- [ ]
- [ ]
- [ ]
- [ ]
- [ ]
- [ ]
- [ ]
- [ ]
- [ ]
- [ ]
- [ ]
- [ ]
- [ ]
- [ ]
- [ ]
- [ ]

*"God, who helps you. . .
who blesses you with
blessings of the skies
above, blessings of the
deep springs below."*

GENESIS 49:25 NIV

September 2022

S	M	T	W	T	F	S
				1	2	3
4	5	6	7	8	9	10
11	12	13	14	15	16	17
18	19	20	21	22	23	24
25	26	27	28	29	30	

God's offer of salvation through the sacrifice of His Son will never be rescinded. His purposeful provision of eternal life for His kids will never be canceled. We can count on it. Rest in it today.

To-Do List

- [ ]
- [ ]
- [ ]
- [ ]
- [ ]
- [ ]
- [ ]
- [ ]
- [ ]
- [ ]
- [ ]
- [ ]
- [ ]
- [ ]
- [ ]
- [ ]
- [ ]
- [ ]
- [ ]

SUNDAY, SEPTEMBER 11

MONDAY, SEPTEMBER 12

TUESDAY, SEPTEMBER 13

WEDNESDAY, SEPTEMBER 14

THURSDAY, SEPTEMBER 15

FRIDAY, SEPTEMBER 16

SATURDAY, SEPTEMBER 17

To-Do List

☐
☐
☐
☐
☐
☐
☐
☐
☐
☐
☐
☐
☐
☐
☐
☐
☐
☐

God's gifts and God's call are under full warranty—never canceled, never rescinded.

ROMANS 11:29 MSG

September 2022

S	M	T	W	T	F	S
				1	2	3
4	5	6	7	8	9	10
11	12	13	14	15	16	17
18	19	20	21	22	23	24
25	26	27	28	29	30	

Each of us has a unique platform from which to tell our own story. Our eternal destiny is secure; let's share the news.

To-Do List

- [ ]
- [ ]
- [ ]
- [ ]
- [ ]
- [ ]
- [ ]
- [ ]
- [ ]
- [ ]
- [ ]
- [ ]
- [ ]
- [ ]
- [ ]
- [ ]
- [ ]
- [ ]
- [ ]

SUNDAY, SEPTEMBER 18

MONDAY, SEPTEMBER 19

TUESDAY, SEPTEMBER 20

WEDNESDAY, SEPTEMBER 21

THURSDAY, SEPTEMBER 22
First Day of Autumn

FRIDAY, SEPTEMBER 23

SATURDAY, SEPTEMBER 24

To-Do List

☐
☐
☐
☐
☐
☐
☐
☐
☐
☐
☐
☐
☐
☐
☐
☐
☐
☐
☐
☐

*"Return home and
tell how much God
has done for you."*

LUKE 8:39 NIV

September 2022

S	M	T	W	T	F	S
				1	2	3
4	5	6	7	8	9	10
11	12	13	14	15	16	17
18	19	20	21	22	23	24
25	26	27	28	29	30	

God's love touches our entire lives. Even better, He pours His love into our very being. We are like a cup that God never stops filling up with His love.

To-Do List

- [ ]
- [ ]
- [ ]
- [ ]
- [ ]
- [ ]
- [ ]
- [ ]
- [ ]
- [ ]
- [ ]
- [ ]
- [ ]
- [ ]
- [ ]
- [ ]
- [ ]
- [ ]
- [ ]

SUNDAY, SEPTEMBER 25

MONDAY, SEPTEMBER 26

TUESDAY, SEPTEMBER 27

WEDNESDAY, SEPTEMBER 28

THURSDAY, SEPTEMBER 29

FRIDAY, SEPTEMBER 30

SATURDAY, OCTOBER 1

To-Do List

- [ ]
- [ ]
- [ ]
- [ ]
- [ ]
- [ ]
- [ ]
- [ ]
- [ ]
- [ ]
- [ ]
- [ ]
- [ ]
- [ ]
- [ ]
- [ ]
- [ ]
- [ ]

*God's love has been
poured out into
our hearts through
the Holy Spirit.*

ROMANS 5:5 NIV

October 2022

SUNDAY	MONDAY	TUESDAY	WEDNESDAY
25	26	27	28
2	3	4	5
9	10 *Columbus Day*	11	12
16	17	18	19
23	24	25	26
30	31 *Halloween*		

Notes

THURSDAY	FRIDAY	SATURDAY
29	30	1
6	7	8
13	14	15
20	21	22
27	28	29

....
....
....
....
....
....
....
....
....
....
....
....

SEPTEMBER

S	M	T	W	T	F	S
				1	2	3
4	5	6	7	8	9	10
11	12	13	14	15	16	17
18	19	20	21	22	23	24
25	26	27	28	29	30	

NOVEMBER

S	M	T	W	T	F	S
		1	2	3	4	5
6	7	8	9	10	11	12
13	14	15	16	17	18	19
20	21	22	23	24	25	26
27	28	29	30			

God's House of Joy

When we feel as though we're too weak to accomplish anything, we often feel blue and depressed. Our self-image suffers. We measure ourselves against others around us and come up lacking. But it doesn't have to be that way. When we stop focusing on our own lack and instead turn our eyes to God, He welcomes us with open arms into His house—a place where joy and strength go hand in hand.

GOALS *for the* MONTH

....
....
....
....
....
....
....
....
....
....
....
....
....
....
....
....
....
....
....
....
....

*Strength and joy are
in his dwelling place.*
1 CHRONICLES 16:27 NIV

October 2022

S	M	T	W	T	F	S
						1
2	3	4	5	6	7	8
9	10	11	12	13	14	15
16	17	18	19	20	21	22
23	24	25	26	27	28	29
30	31					

Using your God-given talents as an investment or to help meet the needs of your family can be a blessing. Beauty is creatively using your gifts for good.

To-Do List

☐
☐
☐
☐
☐
☐
☐
☐
☐
☐
☐
☐
☐
☐
☐
☐
☐
☐
☐

SUNDAY, OCTOBER 2

MONDAY, OCTOBER 3

TUESDAY, OCTOBER 4

WEDNESDAY, OCTOBER 5

THURSDAY, OCTOBER 6

FRIDAY, OCTOBER 7

SATURDAY, OCTOBER 8

To-Do List

She makes linen garments and sells them, and supplies sashes for the merchants.

PROVERBS 31:24 NKJV

October 2022

S	M	T	W	T	F	S
						1
2	3	4	5	6	7	8
9	10	11	12	13	14	15
16	17	18	19	20	21	22
23	24	25	26	27	28	29
30	31					

Our Father in heaven tells
us to bring our desires to Him.
But first, we are to delight ourselves
in Him, find in Him our highest joy.
Then our cravings will be framed by
our desire for His will in us, and the
beauty of that is beyond compare.

To-Do List

☐
☐
☐
☐
☐
☐
☐
☐
☐
☐
☐
☐
☐
☐
☐
☐
☐

SUNDAY, OCTOBER 9

MONDAY, OCTOBER 10 *Columbus Day*

TUESDAY, OCTOBER 11

WEDNESDAY, OCTOBER 12

....
....
....
....
....

THURSDAY, OCTOBER 13

....
....
....
....
....

FRIDAY, OCTOBER 14

....
....
....
....
....

SATURDAY, OCTOBER 15

....
....
....
....
....

To-Do List

- [ ] ....
- [ ] ....
- [ ] ....
- [ ] ....
- [ ] ....
- [ ] ....
- [ ] ....
- [ ] ....
- [ ] ....
- [ ] ....
- [ ] ....
- [ ] ....
- [ ] ....
- [ ] ....
- [ ] ....
- [ ] ....
- [ ] ....
- [ ] ....

*Delight yourself
also in the Lord, and
He will give you the
desires and secret
petitions of your heart.*

PSALM 37:4 AMPC

October 2022

S	M	T	W	T	F	S
						1
2	3	4	5	6	7	8
9	10	11	12	13	14	15
16	17	18	19	20	21	22
23	24	25	26	27	28	29
30	31					

The Word of God is filled with power. It will strengthen you when you need it most.

To-Do List

- ☐ ....
- ☐ ....
- ☐ ....
- ☐ ....
- ☐ ....
- ☐ ....
- ☐ ....
- ☐ ....
- ☐ ....
- ☐ ....
- ☐ ....
- ☐ ....
- ☐ ....
- ☐ ....
- ☐ ....
- ☐ ....
- ☐ ....
- ☐ ....

SUNDAY, OCTOBER 16

MONDAY, OCTOBER 17

TUESDAY, OCTOBER 18

WEDNESDAY, OCTOBER 19

THURSDAY, OCTOBER 20

FRIDAY, OCTOBER 21

SATURDAY, OCTOBER 22

*I have hidden your word
in my heart, that I might
not sin against you.*

PSALM 119:11 NLT

October 2022

S	M	T	W	T	F	S
						1
2	3	4	5	6	7	8
9	10	11	12	13	14	15
16	17	18	19	20	21	22
23	24	25	26	27	28	29
30	31					

God's peace is deeper, wider, and greater than any peace we can imagine. We can't understand it—but we can experience it. It will guard our thoughts and emotions, even in the middle of heartache and trouble.

To-Do List

SUNDAY, OCTOBER 23

MONDAY, OCTOBER 24

TUESDAY, OCTOBER 25

WEDNESDAY, OCTOBER 26

THURSDAY, OCTOBER 27

FRIDAY, OCTOBER 28

SATURDAY, OCTOBER 29

Then you will experience God's peace, which exceeds anything we can understand. His peace will guard your hearts and minds as you live in Christ Jesus.

PHILIPPIANS 4:7 NLT

November 2022

SUNDAY	MONDAY	TUESDAY	WEDNESDAY
30	31	1	2
6 *Daylight Saving Time Ends*	7	8 *Election Day*	9
13	14	15	16
20	21	22	23
27	28	29	30

Notes

THURSDAY	FRIDAY	SATURDAY
3	4	5
10	11 _Veterans Day_	12
17	18	19
24 _Thanksgiving Day_	25	26
1	2	3

OCTOBER

S	M	T	W	T	F	S
						1
2	3	4	5	6	7	8
9	10	11	12	13	14	15
16	17	18	19	20	21	22
23	24	25	26	27	28	29
30	31					

DECEMBER

S	M	T	W	T	F	S
				1	2	3
4	5	6	7	8	9	10
11	12	13	14	15	16	17
18	19	20	21	22	23	24
25	26	27	28	29	30	31

Throw a Party

We serve the Lord when we serve others. The psalmist set the tone for that service when he wrote this song. That word *gladness* in Hebrew reflects the activities associated with the feast days of Israel or a wedding celebration. If we were translating it today, we might say something like: "Let's throw a party and serve the Lord!" Truth is, serving our neighbors or coworkers shouldn't be a chore. Done with the right attitude, it's a celebration!

GOALS *for the* MONTH

Serve the LORD with gladness.
PSALM 100:2 KJV

November 2022

S	M	T	W	T	F	S
		1	2	3	4	5
6	7	8	9	10	11	12
13	14	15	16	17	18	19
20	21	22	23	24	25	26
27	28	29	30			

No circumstance or person will ever be strong enough to push our God out of the way. Even His haters will ultimately bow their knee before His throne. So when the going gets tough, always remember that, in the end, God wins.

To-Do List

- [ ]
- [ ]
- [ ]
- [ ]
- [ ]
- [ ]
- [ ]
- [ ]
- [ ]
- [ ]
- [ ]
- [ ]
- [ ]
- [ ]
- [ ]
- [ ]
- [ ]
- [ ]
- [ ]

SUNDAY, OCTOBER 30

MONDAY, OCTOBER 31 · Halloween

TUESDAY, NOVEMBER 1

WEDNESDAY, NOVEMBER 2

....

....

....

....

....

THURSDAY, NOVEMBER 3

....

....

....

....

....

FRIDAY, NOVEMBER 4

....

....

....

....

....

SATURDAY, NOVEMBER 5

....

....

....

....

....

To-Do List

☐
☐
☐
☐
☐
☐
☐
☐
☐
☐
☐
☐
☐
☐

The suffering won't last forever. It won't be long before this generous God who has great plans for us in Christ—eternal and glorious plans they are!—will have you put together and on your feet for good. He gets the last word; yes, he does.

1 PETER 5:10–11 MSG

November 2022

S	M	T	W	T	F	S
		1	2	3	4	5
6	7	8	9	10	11	12
13	14	15	16	17	18	19
20	21	22	23	24	25	26
27	28	29	30			

If we're patient, even the darkest nights give way to the dawn. God's light will rise in our lives once again—and all the shadows will disappear.

To-Do List

- [ ]
- [ ]
- [ ]
- [ ]
- [ ]
- [ ]
- [ ]
- [ ]
- [ ]
- [ ]
- [ ]
- [ ]
- [ ]
- [ ]
- [ ]
- [ ]
- [ ]
- [ ]

SUNDAY, NOVEMBER 6
Daylight Saving Time Ends

MONDAY, NOVEMBER 7

TUESDAY, NOVEMBER 8 *Election Day*

WEDNESDAY, NOVEMBER 9

THURSDAY, NOVEMBER 10

FRIDAY, NOVEMBER 11 *Veterans Day*

SATURDAY, NOVEMBER 12

To-Do List

☐
☐
☐
☐
☐
☐
☐
☐
☐
☐
☐
☐
☐
☐
☐
☐
☐
☐

"The people living in darkness have seen a great light; on those living in the land of the shadow of death a light has dawned."

MATTHEW 4:16 NIV

November 2022

S	M	T	W	T	F	S
		1	2	3	4	5
6	7	8	9	10	11	12
13	14	15	16	17	18	19
20	21	22	23	24	25	26
27	28	29	30			

It's hard to revel in the beauty of life if we're bogged down with stuff. So the Father tells us to let Him help us carry the load. Today, He wants you to know that you are not alone.

To-Do List

- [ ] ....
- [ ] ....
- [ ] ....
- [ ] ....
- [ ] ....
- [ ] ....
- [ ] ....
- [ ] ....
- [ ] ....
- [ ] ....
- [ ] ....
- [ ] ....
- [ ] ....
- [ ] ....
- [ ] ....
- [ ] ....
- [ ] ....
- [ ] ....
- [ ] ....

SUNDAY, NOVEMBER 13

MONDAY, NOVEMBER 14

TUESDAY, NOVEMBER 15

WEDNESDAY, NOVEMBER 16

THURSDAY, NOVEMBER 17

FRIDAY, NOVEMBER 18

SATURDAY, NOVEMBER 19

To-Do List

*Cast your burden
on the LORD, and He
shall sustain you.*
PSALM 55:22 NKJV

November 2022

S	M	T	W	T	F	S
		1	2	3	4	5
6	7	8	9	10	11	12
13	14	15	16	17	18	19
20	21	22	23	24	25	26
27	28	29	30			

God is always directing our steps in simple ways. Our job is to tune out our heads and tune in to our hearts.

To-Do List

☐
☐
☐
☐
☐
☐
☐
☐
☐
☐
☐
☐
☐
☐
☐
☐
☐
☐
☐

SUNDAY, NOVEMBER 20

MONDAY, NOVEMBER 21

TUESDAY, NOVEMBER 22

WEDNESDAY, NOVEMBER 23

THURSDAY, NOVEMBER 24
Thanksgiving Day

FRIDAY, NOVEMBER 25

SATURDAY, NOVEMBER 26

To-Do List

☐
☐
☐
☐
☐
☐
☐
☐
☐
☐
☐
☐
☐
☐
☐
☐
☐
☐
☐
☐

*"My thoughts are
nothing like your
thoughts," says the LORD.
"And my ways are far
beyond anything you
could imagine."*

ISAIAH 55:8 NLT

November 2022

S	M	T	W	T	F	S
		1	2	3	4	5
6	7	8	9	10	11	12
13	14	15	16	17	18	19
20	21	22	23	24	25	26
27	28	29	30			

We tend to separate the spiritual world from the physical one, but the Bible shows us a perspective where each sort of blessing flows into all the others. As we are spiritually blessed, our physical lives will be blessed as well.

To-Do List

☐
☐
☐
☐
☐
☐
☐
☐
☐
☐
☐
☐
☐
☐
☐
☐
☐
☐
☐
☐

SUNDAY, NOVEMBER 27

MONDAY, NOVEMBER 28

TUESDAY, NOVEMBER 29

WEDNESDAY, NOVEMBER 30

THURSDAY, DECEMBER 1

FRIDAY, DECEMBER 2

SATURDAY, DECEMBER 3

☐
☐
☐
☐
☐
☐
☐
☐
☐
☐
☐
☐
☐
☐
☐
☐

*Beloved, I pray that
in all respects you
may prosper and be
in good health, just
as your soul prospers.*

3 JOHN 2 NASB

December 2022

SUNDAY	MONDAY	TUESDAY	WEDNESDAY
27	28	29	30
4	5	6	7
11	12	13	14
18 *Hanukkah Begins at Sundown*	19	20	21 *First Day of Winter*
25 *Christmas Day*	26	27	28

Notes

THURSDAY	FRIDAY	SATURDAY
1	2	3
8	9	10
15	16	17
22	23	24 *Christmas Eve*
29	30	31 *New Year's Eve*

NOVEMBER

S	M	T	W	T	F	S
		1	2	3	4	5
6	7	8	9	10	11	12
13	14	15	16	17	18	19
20	21	22	23	24	25	26
27	28	29	30			

JANUARY

S	M	T	W	T	F	S
1	2	3	4	5	6	7
8	9	10	11	12	13	14
15	16	17	18	19	20	21
22	23	24	25	26	27	28
29	30	31				

Relentless Love

You can turn your eyes away from God. You can insist on shutting your heart against Him. But God's love is unstoppable and relentless. It leaks into the cracks of your heart. It waits patiently for you to turn around and notice it's there. It is always ready to bless you.

GOALS *for the* MONTH

....

....

....

....

....

....

....

....

....

....

....

....

....

....

....

....

I am convinced that nothing can ever separate us from God's love. Neither death nor life, neither angels nor demons, neither our fears for today nor our worries about tomorrow— not even the powers of hell can separate us from God's love.
ROMANS 8:38 NLT

December 2022

S	M	T	W	T	F	S
				1	2	3
4	5	6	7	8	9	10
11	12	13	14	15	16	17
18	19	20	21	22	23	24
25	26	27	28	29	30	31

God never intended for His kids
to live the solitary life. His plan
is for us to be in a community,
to know others and to be known.

To-Do List

- [ ] ....
- [ ] ....
- [ ] ....
- [ ] ....
- [ ] ....
- [ ] ....
- [ ] ....
- [ ] ....
- [ ] ....
- [ ] ....
- [ ] ....
- [ ] ....
- [ ] ....
- [ ] ....
- [ ] ....
- [ ] ....
- [ ] ....
- [ ] ....

SUNDAY, DECEMBER 4

MONDAY, DECEMBER 5

TUESDAY, DECEMBER 6

WEDNESDAY, DECEMBER 7

THURSDAY, DECEMBER 8

FRIDAY, DECEMBER 9

SATURDAY, DECEMBER 10

To-Do List

*And Ruth said, Intreat
me not to leave thee,
or to return from
following after thee:
for whither thou goest,
I will go; and where
thou lodgest, I will lodge.*

RUTH 1:16 KJV

December 2022

S	M	T	W	T	F	S
				1	2	3
4	5	6	7	8	9	10
11	12	13	14	15	16	17
18	19	20	21	22	23	24
25	26	27	28	29	30	31

When the Bible talks about a covenant, it's referring to a binding promise that can never be broken. God's promise of peace is a solid thing, firm and unchanging. It's a covenant that will never be broken.

To-Do List

- [ ]
- [ ]
- [ ]
- [ ]
- [ ]
- [ ]
- [ ]
- [ ]
- [ ]
- [ ]
- [ ]
- [ ]
- [ ]
- [ ]
- [ ]
- [ ]
- [ ]
- [ ]

SUNDAY, DECEMBER 11

MONDAY, DECEMBER 12

TUESDAY, DECEMBER 13

WEDNESDAY, DECEMBER 14

THURSDAY, DECEMBER 15

FRIDAY, DECEMBER 16

SATURDAY, DECEMBER 17

To-Do List

I give unto him my covenant of peace.
NUMBERS 25:12 KJV

December 2022

S	M	T	W	T	F	S
				1	2	3
4	5	6	7	8	9	10
11	12	13	14	15	16	17
18	19	20	21	22	23	24
25	26	27	28	29	30	31

Just as quickly as negative circumstances come into our lives, we can always remind ourselves that anything can happen. God can turn our lives around in moments. Keep focused on Him; He will bring you through.

To-Do List

- ☐
- ☐
- ☐
- ☐
- ☐
- ☐
- ☐
- ☐
- ☐
- ☐
- ☐
- ☐
- ☐
- ☐
- ☐
- ☐
- ☐
- ☐
- ☐

SUNDAY, DECEMBER 18
Hanukkah Begins at Sundown

MONDAY, DECEMBER 19

TUESDAY, DECEMBER 20

WEDNESDAY, DECEMBER 21
First Day of Winter

....
....
....
....
....

THURSDAY, DECEMBER 22

....
....
....
....
....

FRIDAY, DECEMBER 23

....
....
....
....
....

SATURDAY, DECEMBER 24
Christmas Eve

....
....
....
....

To-Do List

- [ ] ....
- [ ] ....
- [ ] ....
- [ ] ....
- [ ] ....
- [ ] ....
- [ ] ....
- [ ] ....
- [ ] ....
- [ ] ....
- [ ] ....
- [ ] ....
- [ ] ....
- [ ] ....
- [ ] ....
- [ ] ....
- [ ] ....
- [ ] ....

*You did it: you changed
wild lament into whirling
dance; you ripped off
my black mourning band
and decked me with
wildflowers.*

PSALM 30:11 MSG

December 2022

S	M	T	W	T	F	S
				1	2	3
4	5	6	7	8	9	10
11	12	13	14	15	16	17
18	19	20	21	22	23	24
25	26	27	28	29	30	31

Though our vision isn't what God can see, even our earthly eyes can recognize that we are being transformed a little more every day into a reflection of Him. Through His grace, through our trials and testings, through our faith, we are being conformed to His beautiful image.

To-Do List

- [ ]
- [ ]
- [ ]
- [ ]
- [ ]
- [ ]
- [ ]
- [ ]
- [ ]
- [ ]
- [ ]
- [ ]
- [ ]
- [ ]
- [ ]
- [ ]
- [ ]
- [ ]
- [ ]

SUNDAY, DECEMBER 25 *Christmas Day*

MONDAY, DECEMBER 26

TUESDAY, DECEMBER 27

WEDNESDAY, DECEMBER 28

....

....

....

....

....

THURSDAY, DECEMBER 29

....

....

....

....

....

FRIDAY, DECEMBER 30

....

....

....

....

....

SATURDAY, DECEMBER 31
New Year's Eve

....

....

....

....

To-Do List

- [ ]
- [ ]
- [ ]
- [ ]
- [ ]
- [ ]
- [ ]
- [ ]
- [ ]
- [ ]
- [ ]
- [ ]
- [ ]

But we all, with unveiled face, beholding as in a mirror the glory of the Lord, are being transformed into the same image from glory to glory, just as by the Spirit of the Lord.

2 CORINTHIANS 3:18 NKJV

Notes

Notes

....

....

....

....

....

....

....

....

....

....

....

....

....

....

....

Notes

Notes

....

....

....

....

....

....

....

....

....

....

....

....

....

....

Notes

Notes

....

....

....

....

....

....

....

....

....

....

....

....

....

....

....

....

CONTACTS

Name:

Address:

Phone: Cell:

Email:

Name:

Address:

Phone: Cell:

Email:

Name:

Address:

Phone: Cell:

Email:

Name:

Address:

Phone: Cell:

Email:

CONTACTS

Name:

Address:

Phone: Cell:

Email:

Name:

Address:

Phone: Cell:

Email:

Name:

Address:

Phone: Cell:

Email:

Name:

Address:

Phone: Cell:

Email:

CONTACTS

Name:

Address:

Phone: Cell:

Email:

Name:

Address:

Phone: Cell:

Email:

Name:

Address:

Phone: Cell:

Email:

Name:

Address:

Phone: Cell:

Email:

CONTACTS

Name:

Address:

Phone: Cell:

Email:

Name:

Address:

Phone: Cell:

Email:

Name:

Address:

Phone: Cell:

Email:

Name:

Address:

Phone: Cell:

Email:

CONTACTS

Name:

Address:

Phone: Cell:

Email:

Name:

Address:

Phone: Cell:

Email:

Name:

Address:

Phone: Cell:

Email:

Name:

Address:

Phone: Cell:

Email:

CONTACTS

Name:

Address:

Phone: Cell

Email:

Name:

Address:

Phone: Cell:

Email:

Name:

Address:

Phone: Cell:

Email:

Name:

Address:

Phone: Cell:

Email:

CONTACTS

Name:

Address:

Phone: Cell:

Email:

Name:

Address:

Phone: Cell:

Email:

Name:

Address:

Phone: Cell:

Email:

Name:

Address:

Phone: Cell

Email:

CONTACTS

Name:

Address:

Phone: Cell:

Email:

Name:

Address:

Phone: Cell:

Email:

Name:

Address:

Phone: Cell:

Email:

Name:

Address:

Phone: Cell:

Email:

CONTACTS

Name:

Address:

Phone: Cell:

Email:

Name:

Address:

Phone: Cell:

Email:

Name:

Address:

Phone: Cell:

Email:

Name:

Address:

Phone: Cell:

Email: